Pathak

# INFORMATION MANAGEMENT IN ARCHIVES AND LIBRARIES

# INFORMATION MANAGEMENT IN ARCHIVES AND LIBRARIES

A.R. SINGH

AAKAR PUBLICATIONS

INFORMATION MANAGEMENT
IN ARCHIVES AND LIBRARIES



First Published, 2001

ISBN # 81-87879-01-7

*Published by*
**AAKAR PUBLICATIONS**
28-E, Pocket-IV, Mayur Vihar, Phase-I, Delhi-110 091
Phone : 2716654, 2719249 Telefax : 2711932
E-mail : aakarb@del2.vsnl.net.in

*Laser Typesetting*
Nidhi Laser Point, Shahdara Delhi-32
Ph. : 2825424

*Printed by*
Nidhi Enterprises, Shahdara Delhi-32
E-mail : nidhi_vatsa@hotmail.com

# Preface

The aim of this book is to compare the activities and various operations of library and archives services with special reference to information management, information retrieval, networking, relations between archives and libraries, role of archivists and librarians towards fulfilment of right to information and special role of National Archives of India in providing requisite information to the researchers, decision makers, etc.

An effort has been made to study the management techniques adopted by archivists and librarians, which is to provide comprehensive and need based information to its clienteles.

The expectations that the library and archives professionals equip themselves with adequate professional knowledge and skills for designing, developing, organising, controlling and evaluating systems and services have thrown new challenges for them.

For the fulfilment of the above goals, they have to co-operate with each other to cater to the needs of their clients, as the librarians and archivists will benefit greatly from each others experiences. In this regard, librarians can study archivists methods of content description; and archivists can study standard format, indexing language and thesaurus construction, to which librarians and information scientists have given so much attention.

Chapter 1 provides information management techniques adopted by archives and libraries with special reference to India.

Chapter 2 describes methods of building collections for archival libraries, which is expected to provide secondary information to those researchers, who come to consult Government Records. Most of the researchers come to the library to supplement primary information from published materials.

Chapter 3 gives an inkling of information retrieval techniques followed by archives and archival libraries in India.

Chapter 4 describes the problems and prospect of networking among archives and archival libraries in India.

Chapter 5 makes an attempt to study the affinity between archives and libraries with special reference to accessibility, collections, services to the clienteles, public relations, manpower planning, etc.

Chapter 6 deals with the concept of right to information of the information seekers and the special role being played by the National Archives of India Library in fulfilling their aspirations.

Chapter 7 mentions the role of National Archives of India Library in furnishing requisite information desired by researchers, decision makers, legislatures, judiciary, etc.

I would like to thank my colleagues in National Archives of India, particularly Shri Santi Sarkar and Smt. S. Tyagi who helped me in writing this book by providing requisite information from time to time. I would also like to thank Dr. R.K. Singh and Smt. Pushpa Singh who helped me in preparation of the manuscript for publication.

I hope this book will be useful for the archivists and librarians who want to know the similarity of both the professions and want to gain from the experiences of each other in providing better services to their respective clienteles.

***A.R. Singh***

# Contents

*Chapter 1*

# Information Management in Archives and Libraries in India

## 0 Information

Information is the most precious resource or input for development—economic, social, cultural, spiritual and political. The economic progress of a country can be gauged by the priority and proportion of budget allocation made to the R&D. Exchange of Scientific and Technical information, have played a leading part in historical development of the industrial societies. Advances in knowledge are the result of the two-way flow of information among the scientists and the engineers or again between latter and those who are potentially capable of benefiting from such advances or of putting them in use.

## 1. Managing Information Resources

An efficient modern information management should be able to guarantee that virtually any document in the universe of available literature or any data contained in documents should be accessible to any member of the user community served. This implies that the 'Universe of Document Resources' should be available to the user population of different levels of accessibility. Since no library and information centre can own everything, it is important that the document that it does add to its collection have the greatest probability of being of value to its own users. It is also important, however, that the information centre should be able to acquire, as rapidly as possible, any other document for which there is a legitimate need in the user community, through purchase, photocopying or inter-library loan. Moreover, in the centre's own collections, documents need to be organised according to expected levels of demand, those most likely to be used being most accessible.

## *1.1 In Archives*

The archives and records form an essential and significant part of a nation's information resources and that programmes for their management and use are, or should be, an integral part of the national information system. The archives and record services deal with information bearing materials generated within the administrative system of important organisations (whether government or private institutions or organisations), while on the whole, library and documentation services deal with information bearing materials brought in from outside. To play their part, it is essential that the archives and the record services should operate efficiently within the limitations of available resources. This is all the more true as these services come under greater pressure because of increasing volume of records produced coinciding with the expansion of demand for access to the information in them. Modern records and archives services have to deal with a vast amount of materials, and have to find ways of exploiting their information contents under the constraints of a budget which is never generous, has probably been subjected in recent years to new restrictions.

### *1.2 In Library and Information Centres*

For effective information planning, the librarian or information officer should know something about his clients. Every library has a unique population to serve, the librarian want to know who, of this potential population, use library services; which services they use, how frequently and for what purpose; whether and how non-users can be drawn into the library's sphere of influence. He will also be curious about how the library fits into the general pattern of information flow and communication. The answer to all these queries will be specific to the library in question. Public libraries have a wider audience than any other type of library; yet even here, different libraries play different roles. A small branch library, for example, encounters demands which are of a different nature from those put to a large reference library. Academic libraries cater principally to the students and the staff, with occasional stray members of the general public crossing their threshold. Special libraries have yet more select clientele, although their scope is broader than is sometimes supposed.

## 2. Strategy of Information Planning

Users have different levels of requirement according to their disciplines, concepts of values and roles in society. Until users draw upon this body of records and knowledge, it can not be said to be information in any dynamic sense; custodians down the centuries have sought both to preserve these resources and make them available at the same time. However, 'making available' in terms of physical access must be distinguished from intellectual access. The emphasis is placed, in the first instance, on the basic needs of the individual as a person rather than on the enquiry, then the body of knowledge of record ceases to be a 'scientifically' impersonal objective entity. It has been argued that science is neither autonomous nor self-regulating, but it is essentially a creature and creation of the scientist arising from the activities which closely resemble those of librarian and archivists, who also solve problems, ask question, pursue intuition, formulate hypothesis, test check and verify findings, seek to enlarge generalisation, devise methods and techniques and collect the history and records of the profession.

## 2.1 *User's Requirement*

Librarians have traditionally sought to assist the users in two ways. The first is by providing an end-product in the shape of information required by the users. This is reference work whereby all necessary citations, monographs and similar material are placed before the reader. The second is by providing guidance to readers through the various retrieval systems but essentially leaving to the reader the responsibility for finding the required material. Libraries and archives have much in common concerning user needs, but in addition there are special problems which to a large extent are limited to archives. Archives are created organically by persons and institutions in the course of their affairs, for their own purpose and not primarilly for the use of others. What librarians often call 'government documents' such as printed annual reports of department are also archival materials selected for immediate use and information of the general public through publication and, as such, became library material although with some problems of retrieval in common with original records.

## 2.2 *Assessing the Needs*

Librarians have traditionally been functioning as information transfer agents. They have gathered up data, stored it and awaited for someone to come along who wanted to know. Today we are faced with a society dependent upon a technology which thrives on speed and with that speed goes social change. And if society cannot find the information it needs to know to meet the accelerated pace of decision-making, technology becomes useless. To cater to the needs of their clients, librarians and archivists will benefit greatly from each others experience. In this regard librarians can study archivist's methods of content description, and archivists can study about standard format, indexing language and thesaurus constru-ction to which librarians and information scientists have given so much attention. So far there have been few studies by archivists of user needs and behaviour. With their emphasis on arrangement, they have tended to work outwards from the textual construct which is still largely descriptive of bureaucratic artefacts. They give a service that more or less satisfies their clients, but that is because without further study there is no way that any of them can know how much better they could be.

## 3. Uses of Information for Decision–Making

It is well accepted that the modern age belongs to science and technology. Hence information technology plays a major and vital role in achieving social, culture, political and economic goals of every country. There is no doubt that information has an impact on virtually every facets of our daily lives including our work, leisure, transportation, communication and general welfare. Scientific information embodies not only the heritage of men's verified knowledge, but also the current records. It constitutes an essential resource for the work of scientist. Accordingly, judicious utilisation of information as a national resource is the key to progress in technically advanced or advancing societies. Information involves reduction of uncertainty, that is what the decision maker expects from the information system. However, the degree of uncertainty of the decision maker will vary, and so the amount of information needed or taken from the system will vary. Information is thus a relative quantity, and can be quantified in terms of its effect on the state of the decision maker at a particular moment of time. Records and archives also provide the information that is required by those who make the decisions. The question only is whether these records are available to these decision makers and whether the decision makers are aware of their existence and thus make use of them in making decisions.

### *3.1 Levels of Decision–Making*

The need for decision–making at all levels of management on a continuing basis and providing needed information to decision makers is widely recognised despite complexities involved in meeting all of the needs of the decision makers. There are three levels of decision making viz:

#### *3.1.1 Strategic Level*

Strategic decisions are characterised by a great deal

of uncertainty and are future oriented. They establish long-range plans which affect the entire organisation. The goals of the organisation are stated and a range of strategies is made.

*3.1.2. Tactical Level*

Tactical decision–making pertains to short-term activities and the allocation of resources for the attainment of the objectives. This kind of decision making relates to such areas as formulation of budgets, funds flow analysis, deciding on plan layout, personnel problems, product improvement, and research and development.

*3.1.3 Technical Level*

At this level of decision–making, standards are fixed and results of decisions are deterministic. Technical decision–making is a process of ensuring that specific tasks are implemented in an effective and efficient manner. This kind of decision–making requires specific commands to be given to control specific operations. The primary management function is control, with planning performed on a rather limited scale.

## 4. File Management and Imaging System

In the modern world, information is of capital importance for all countries. It is recognised as essential to social progress and to the understanding of the problems affecting the lives of nations. As administrative structures and organisational framework differ from one country to another, there is neither a standard pattern of planning and implementing information policy, nor ideal or model services and institutes which are needed in each country. Accordingly institutional and legal infrastructures necessary for retrieval and dissemination of information can not be standardised but generalisations are possible to manage information in archives and libraries and to cater to the needs of their respective clients. The archivists in the national archives should store and retrieve information in records deposited for permanent preservation. In addition to this, officials who will be in charge of records administration, the government special librarians, documentalists and information scientists should work in liaison with personnel indicated above to repackage primary, raw published or duplicated information flowed into their information centres. The personnel involved in retrieving and disseminating information should be professionally trained. If the suitable infrastructure does not exist in a particular country, it is advisable to set up at least the basic institutional personnel structure in order to operate a basic information retrieval and disseminating system. This basic structure include the administration of current files in the creating agencies, the identification and retrieval of non-current records containing valuable information in the creating agencies, and the transferring of these records to a national archives for permanent preservation. The imaging tools should also form part of the infrastructure.

## 4.1 Existing Tools

### 4.1.1 Paper

Loose papers have always presented a problem. If they are left loose they can too easily be lost, damaged or mislaid. If they are bound into volumes, it is hard to change their order or to make insertion or removals, without destroying the binding while a series of papers of varying sizes makes a very unsatisfactory binding. This awareness has brought to the force the need for a process of filing loose documents which will meet the requirement of custodial institutions. The process of 'guarding and filing' has, therefore, been developed to avoid not only the disadvantages encountered in keeping papers in loose form or bound into volumes but also to give aesthetic appearance to the finished product. Archival institutions hold large collections of loose papers of the early period. Most of these papers are kept folded and some of them have been bound into volumes.

### 4.1.2 Micrographics

Micrographics have come to play an important role in many aspects of information management, and reliance on these technological tools will undoubtedly continue to increase indefinitely. The use of this technology to disseminate information has placed versatile new tools in the hands of information managers whose objectives after all is to make the storage and handling of information less costly and more efficient. Micrographics play a unique role in maintenance of records, as a means of providing security copies, and as a tool for reducing information storage requirements.

### *4.2 Electronic System*

#### *4.2.1 Magnetic Media*

Magnetic tape has been the basic file medium for virtually every major computer; it provides efficient storage and high-speed transfer rate desired; it is erasable; so the stored data can be changed; its use has been well developed in both numerical computation and business processing.

#### *4.2.2 Optical Media*

An optical disc is next of kin to a video disk. Binary digits are stored on this medium optically (using laser light) rather than magnetically. Optical disks store information with much higher density than magnetic disk do, and they provide extremely rapid access. Nearly all optical disks now in use are of read only memory type but a great deal of research is currently underway. This technology has great promise for dynamic record keeping systems as well as archival storage of information. Optical storage is now being packed in other forms besides disks. These include cartridges, cards, etc.

## *4.3 Integrated System*

The integrated system involves a re-examination of the primary publication process. Primary journals attempt to convey both detailed information on an individual subject speciality, and more general information on broader subjects. The primary journal has long been recognised to be inefficient in providing both these types of information, whether in a current awareness or in archival context. With the information explosion, journals have proliferated in narrower and narrower subject fields, thus increasing the reader's problem of keeping track of all the literature, while lowering the saleable number of copies of each periodical. With such a situation some integrated system of primary publication formats are required to be explored.

## 5. Economic Consideration

Economic considerations must be taken into account while developing information management systems, which should be on the lines on which industries are being managed. In other words, cost of managing information should not be more in comparison to benefit which is likely to accrue to the users of information. Any country, howsoever rich it may be, has limited resources at its disposal and can not afford to ignore the economic considerations of managing information, which is a national resource.

### 5.1 *Cost–Effective Strategies*

Cost–effective strategies for developing information management systems should play a dominant role as information being a national resource, is required to be managed on the pattern of industries. Cost–benefit considerations are to be allowed to play in full as public money is involved. The cost of managing information should not be more than that of users benefit assessed in terms of money. However, in developing countries, specially in the case of information managed by archives and records centres, cost-effective strategies should not be adhered to till a consciousness regarding value of archival information, which is primary one in nature, is created among the users, specially managed by libraries and information centres.

## 6. Conclusion

To provide right information to the right reader, at the right time in the right amount and in the right form should be the motto of information managers of libraries and information centres including archives and record centres. The traditional archival information services are required to be replaced by modern techniques of documentation and dissemination of information. Modernisation implies the advent of sophisticated techniques to control information and application of automated information methods for the dissemination.

*Chapter 2*

# Archival Libraries Collection Development

## 1. Archival Libraries: Nature and Scope of their Collection

The main functions of National Archives of India and State Government's Archives are to collect, preserve and organise Government's records and other materials of historical importance. National Archives of India being an apex archival institution of the country is generally expected to provide technical know-how and requisite training to the professionals of state and other archival institutions. With the growth of concept of preservation of cultural heritage of the country as well as that of the various regions, the archives are expected to inculcate the awareness about preservation of old cultural heritage among public at large. National Archives of India as well as various state archives mount exhibitions and organise lectures and celebrate archives week for the fulfillment of this objective.

Though the main clienteles of the archives are decision makers of the Central and State Governments, but in recent years the main thrust is shifting towards the researchers, who come to the archives to consult the records created by various Ministries of the Government, in the pursuit of their researches. The National Archives of India is running various training programs ranging from short durations to one year Diploma course in Archives Keeping, with the objective to provide technical knowledge to the individuals and organizations interested in records management, preservation, reprography etc.

The main objective of the National Archives of India library is to cater to the requirements of creators of the records of the Governments of India, Legislators, Judiciary, decision-makers, bonafide research scholars of the Universities of India and abroad, trainees of various short term as well as one year courses run by the School of Archival Studies, authors, writers, etc. The library provides secondary sources of information and functions as a useful adjunct to the Govt. of India records available in the National Archives of India.

Keeping in view the specific requirements of the aforesaid clienteles, the collection of the National Archives of India library holding mainly consists of the under mentioned publication, which is being continuously enriched by adding reference books and source materials on Modern Indian History:

## I. *Gazettes*

| | |
|---|---|
| (*i*) Calcutta Gazette, 1792-1863<br>(*ii*) India Gazette, 1864-<br>(*iii*) London Gazette, 1810-1954 | with gaps |

The Gazette of India is unique collection in the holdings of this library, which gives information relating to the acts passed by the Indian Parliament, orders and appointments, notified by the various ministries and departments for the information of public at large. The Calcutta and London Gazettes give valuable information about the activities of the then British Government.

## II. *Gazetteers*

(*i*) Imperial Gazetteer of India (India Series)

(*ii*) Imperial Gazetteer of India (Provincial Series)

(*iii*) District Gazetteers of India published since its very inception.

The Gazetteer give valuable information about the people of India, their customs, culture, history and geographical details of various places of the country. The statistical details are also available in its Part 2.

## III. *Census of India/State/Districts, 1871—*

The information contains on caste, tribes and other population relating to their material being including education, income, literacy, etc. These are the primary source material for the study of demography of the country. Prior to 1941 censuses, the data about various castes and sub-castes were also collected. However, this practice was discontinued after 1931 Census.

### *IV. Administrative reports of Indian Union and its States and Territories, 1855-1933 (with gaps)*

These publications deal with administration, politics, economic affairs, foreign affairs, tackling of law and orders by the governments.

### *V. Parliamentary Debates*

These are the proceedings of the House of Commons and House of Lords, wherein the debates on Indian affairs also took place. From the perusal of the debates, it is noticed that sometime lively discussion took place, in which conditions of Indian subjects was debated. A number of white papers presented to British Parliament on the affairs of India are available in the library. A very important series viz. moral and material progress of Indian people, which was placed before the Parliament also forms part of the precious collection of the library.

Some of the important publications in the series are given hereunder:

(*i*) Cobett's Parliamentary History of England, 1066-1803

(*ii*) The Mirror of Parliament, 1829-1839

(*iii*) Hansard's Parliamentary Debates, 1842-1891

(*iv*) Hansard's Parliamentary Debates relating to Indian Affairs, 1886-1925

(*v*) Parliamentary Debates, 1892-1935
(*vi*) Indian Parliamentary Debates, 1892-1898
(*vii*) Indian Debates, 1898-1908
(*viii*) Debates on Indian Affairs, 1909-1935.

### VI. *Legislative Assembly Debates*

(*i*) Proceedings of the Legislative Council of India, 1857-1920
(*ii*) Legislative Assembly Debates of Indian Legislatures, 1921-1947
(*iii*) Constituent Assembly Debates, 1947-1950
(*iv*) Parliamentary Debates, 1947-1950
(*v*) Rajya Sabha Debates, 1952-
(*vi*) Lok Sabha Debates, 1954-

These are the proceedings of the then Legislative Council of India and Legislative Assembly Debates of then Indian Legislatures, now known as Lok Sabha and Rajya Sabha Debates. The collection includes constituent assembly and parliamentary debates.

### VII. *Provincial Legislative Council Debates*

These are the proceedings of the Legislative Councils of various provinces prior to reorganisation of the Indian states. The holdings are given hereunder:

| | | |
|---|---|---|
| (*i*) Bengal | 1862-1932 | |
| (*ii*) Bombay | 1862-1936 | |
| (*iii*) Burma | 1923-1935 | |
| (*iv*) Central Provinces | 1916-1932 | with |
| (*v*) Madras | 1922-1936 | gaps |

(*vi*) Punjab 1926-1936
(*vii*) United Provinces 1896-1936

## *VIII. India Office List*

It contains the service records of the officers, who served in India and Burma, especially those officers, who were in all India and Burma class I services.

## *IX. India Army List*

In this list, the names of the army officers, their postings, date of joining of the army, ranks and positions are mentioned. There are also following lists as well, which gives the similar information relating to Bengal, Bombay and Madras Armies:

(*i*) Bengal Army List —1825-1889
(*ii*) Bombay Army List—1826-1895 with gaps
(*iii*) Madras Army List—1826-1894

## *X. Civil List, 1886-1989 (with gaps)*

This list provides complete data about the officers of the Indian service as well as Indian Administrative Services.

## *XI. Selections of Vernacular Native Newspapers, 1863-1937 (with gaps)*

These are the abstracts or summary of political news, which were published in vernacular native newspaper during British Rule. The objective was to get the British Rulers informed about the political mood of the Indians, who were fighting for freedom of the country. These reports were compiled by Home Department. Each provinces had translators, who translated the reportings from native languages to English. The series is primary source material for the study of march towards freedom as it reflected the public opinion of various provinces regarding British administration. Prior to independence, these selections were classified as confidential documents, and were not meant for public information.

Some important reports available in the series are as under:

(*i*) Report on Native Newspapers, Bengal Presidency, 1863-1931 (with gaps)

(*ii*) Report on Native Newspapers, Bombay Presidency, 1868-1932 (with gaps)

(*iii*) Report on Native Newspapers, Central Provinces, Merwara, Central India, etc., 1896-1927 (with gaps)

(*iv*) Report on the Native Newspapers, Eastern Bengal and Assam, 1907-1911 (with gaps)

(*v*) Report on Native Newspapers, Madras, 1872-1911 (with gaps)

(*vi*) Report on Native Newspapers, North-Western Provinces and Oudh (Awadh), 1890-1937 (with gaps)

### *XII. Selection from Records*

These records are selections of important activities of the then British government. These were published for use and information of public at large. The selected records pertain to the important aspects of British administration in India. Notable among these are the following selections of India and its States:

(*i*) Selections from records of the Government of India, 1853-1900 (with gaps)

(*ii*) Selections from records of the Bengal Government, 1851-1890 (with gaps)

(*iii*) Selections from records of the Bombay Government, 1852-1907 (with gaps)

(*iv*) Selections from records of the Punjab Government, 1852-1879 (with gaps)

(*v*) Selections from records of the Madras Government, 1853-1896 (with gaps)

### XIII. East India Register and Directory

These provide complete information about servants of East India Company, who were employed in its civil, military, and marine establishments.

### XIV. Times of India Directory, 1865-1983 (with gaps)

It gives information about Indian population, trade and commerce, organizations of Indian Union and States. It also, provides biographical details of important persons.

### XV. Almanacs

These contain statistical account, astronomical data, Indian events, information relating to civil and military appointments, rules, regulations and notifications of Government of India, etc. The availability is as follows:

| | | | |
|---|---|---|---|
| (*i*) | Bengal Almanac | - 1803-1854 | with gaps |
| (*ii*) | Bombay Calendar and Almanac | - 1836-1868 | |
| (*iii*) | Madras Almanac | - 1827-1858 | |
| (*v*) | Asylum Press Almanac | - 1862-1958 | |

***XVI. Collection of Treaties, Engagements and Sanads compiled by C.U. Aitchison, 14 Volumes, 1900-1929***

These are the compilation of treaties in between princely Indian States and the countries in the neighbourhood of India and East India Company.

***XVII. Annual Register (Great Britain), 1877-1988 (with gaps)***

Gives events of Great Britain and its Colonies and also that of Europe in chronological order. Besides, mentioning history, politics, literature, etc., of England and Europe.

***XVIII. Indian Annual Register, 1919-1947 (with gaps)***

It provides information relating to India on politics, sociology, education, industrial development and public activities.

## XIX. Proscribed Literature

These are in the form of prose, poetry, pamphlets and posters. These publications were brought out in almost all the Indian native languages and also in English, especially during British Raj. The objective of the writers/publishers had been to arouse patriotic fervour in the minds of the Indian masses regarding atrocities committed by the British rulers; and to invoke them to contribute their might to get the motherland liberated from the British oppressors. The British Rulers reacted by banning the publication to ensure that the publications may not reach the people at large. A few notable publications from the series are as follows:

(*i*) *Azadi Ka Bigul* (Hindi), edited by K. C. Rastogi

(*ii*) *Azadi Ka Bomb* (Hindi), edited by Jagannath Prasad Arora

(*iii*) *Kanavu* (Tamil), by Subramaniya Bharati

A few publications based on the material relating to patriotic fervour portrayed in banned publications have been selected and published in the form of books for the benefit of the people and researchers. These are as follows:

(*i*) Patriotic Poetry banned by the Raj

(*ii*) Patriotic Writings banned by the Raj

(*iii*) Deshbhakti Ke Geet (Hindi)

(*iv*) Azadi Ke Tarane (Hindi and Urdu)

(*v*) Dharti Ki Pukar (Hindi)

## *XX. Fort William—India House Correspondence*

(*i*) *Fort William—India House Correspondence*, Volume XIV: (Foreign, Secret, Select Committee, 1752-1781), edited by Amba Prasad (Delhi, 1987).

(*ii*) *Fort William—India House Correspondence*, Volume XV: (Foreign and Secret, 1782-1786), edited by C.H. Philips and B.B. Misra (Delhi, 1963).

(*iii*) *Fort William—India House Correspondence*, Volume XVI: (Foreign, Secret and Political, 1787-1791), edited by Syed Hasan Askari (Delhi, 1976).

(*iv*) *Fort William—India House Correspondence*, Volume XVII: (Foreign, Political and Secret, 1792-1795), edited by Y.J. Taraporewala (Delhi, 1955).

(*v*) *Fort William—India House Correspondence*, Volume XVIII: (Foreign, Political and Secret, 1796-1800), edited by Rev. Father H. Heras (Delhi, 1955).

(*vi*) *Fort William—India House Correspondence*, Volume XIX: (Military, 1797-1791), edited by Bisheshwar Prasad, (Delhi, 1975).

(*vii*) *Fort William—India House Correspondence*, Volume XX: (Military, 1792-1796), edited by A.C. Banerjee (Delhi, 1969).

(*viii*) *Fort William—India House Correspondence*, Volume XXI: (Military, 1797-1800), edited by Amba Prasad, (Delhi, 1969).

### *XXI. A Fort William College Collection*

These are the rare and out of print books transferred from Fort William to the then Imperial Record Department, now National Archives of India. The publications are on variety of subjects, like holy scriptures, customs and traditions of India, biography of eminent persons, travel accounts, history, geography, language and literature. In the collection, commentaries of subject specialists particularly on scriptures, traditions, etc., are also available.

A few publications under this category are as follows:

(*i*) *Mathnawi Bahr-i-Gham* by Sayyid Abu Tayyab Khan

(*ii*) *Zafarnamah* by Maulana Sharf-al-din Ali Yezdi

To facilitate the study of publications in oriental languages, like Urdu, Persian and Arabic, the Department had brought out the two catalogues, viz.:

(*i*) Catalogue of Books of the Fort William College Collection in the National Archives of India Library, and

(*ii*) Catalogue of Manuscripts of the Fort William College Collection in the National Archives of India Library.

### *XXI. Travel Accounts*

These are the first-hand account of the foreign travellers, who travelled from one part to the other part of India and also neighbouring countries. In their narratives, they had depicted the lifestyle, customs, as well as social hierarchy and economic well-being of the masses of different parts visited by them.

A few notable accounts are as follows:

(*i*) Travels in the Himalayan Provinces of Hindustan and the Punjab; in Ladakh and Kashmir; in Peshawar, Kabul by William Moorcroft (1841).

(*ii*) Journals kept in Hyderabad, Kashmir, Sikkim and Nepal by Richard Temple (1887).

In the series, Hakluyt Society had published voyages, travels, naval expeditions and geographical records of personalities. A large number of the publications of the society forms part of the precious collection of National Archives of India Library.

### *XXII. Freedom Struggle Papers/Books*

These gives a vivid account of march towards freedom. A few notable publications available on the subject are as follow:

(*i*) *Press List of Mutiny Papers (1921)*

(*ii*) *History of the Indian Mutiny* by G.W. Forrest (1893)

(*iii*) *Communism in India (1924-1927)*

(*iv*) *India and Communism (1933)*

(*v*) *Histories of Non-Cooperation and Khilafat Movements* by P.C. Bamford (1925)

### XXIII. *Journals and Bulletins*

These are the core journals for the study of the history and culture of the Indian people. A glimpse of traditions and customs are reflected in the journals and bulletins. A few notable among these are:

(*i*) *Calcutta Review*, 1944-1957

(*ii*) *Asiatic Researches*, 1788-1839

(*iii*) *Journal of the Asiatic Society of Bengal*, 1836-1905

(*iv*) *Modern Review*, 1911 - -

(*v*) *Bengal Past and Present*, 1907 - -

(*vi*) *Epigraphica Indica*, 1897-1975

(*vii*) *Indian Antiquary*, 1873-1874, 1943-1944

(*viii*) *Bulletin of the Institute of Historical Research*, 1926 - -

(*ix*) *Bulletin of the School of Oriental and African Studies*, 1944 - -

### XXIV. *Newspapers*

The library is in possession of *Kesari* newspaper, which is preserved because of its rarity. The other newspaper preserved in the Library is *London Times*, the availability of each is mentioned below:

(*i*) *Kesari*, 1913-1953

(*ii*) *London Times*, 1896-1946

## 1.1 *Organisational Goals to be Met by the Collection*

Like other Libraries the collection of National Archives of India Library is also being continuously built keeping in view the information requirements of its users. The making of an effective collection to attain the set goal of the department which is a national institution responsible for collection, preserving and providing Government of India records for reference and research, is a continuous process. However, in recent years the shadow of economic recession is being cast in collection building which is likely to affect acquisition of useful publications.

## 2. *Impact of Economic Recession on Archival Libraries in India*

The economic recession has cast its shadow on almost all national activity. But its effect on Libraries is seen to be maximum as libraries were already starved of working funds for purchasing/subscribing books and periodicals. The effect of economic recession resulted in cut in purchases of useful publications by archival libraries; and also discontinuance of certain periodicals.

### *2.1 National Archives of India Library*

National Archives Library is comparatively in better position as it receives a large number of government publications free of cost. Further, it receives most of the archival periodicals under exchange programmes and by virtue of being a institutional member of a number of national and international organisations. It also receives publication's on complimentary basis and also as gift from eminent personalities. These methods of collection development checks the effects of recession.

### 2.2 *State Archives Libraries*

The State Archival Libraries are not fortunate enough as National Archives of India Library is, in regard to receipt of free publications as their area of influence is limited to respective states. But, they too receive publications through some means, other than purchase. They are, therefore, having marginal effect of economic recession in their collection-building programmes.

## 3. Archival Libraries Collection Development

### 3.1 *Policies*

Uptil now, the National archives of India Library and state archives libraries were depending on their own resources for purchasing/subscribing books and periodicals. None has given any thought to cooperative collection-building processes. There has also not been any effort to avoid duplication of purchases either by National Archives of India Library or State Archives Libraries as such, which is resulting in avoidable expenditure on purchase of books and periodicals. In view of the effect of economic recession, the archival libraries must change their policies of collection development.

### 3.2 *Plans and Programmes*

Archival libraries should evolve some sort of

mechanism and devise suitable plans and programmes of collection development to combat economic recession and safeguard user's interests. For the purpose, State Archives Libraries and National Archives of India Library can join together and go for joint acquisition of publications including periodicals and ensure optimum utilisation of resources at their disposal as these are never generous. The area of subject of purchase to be clearly earmarked to avoid duplication in purchase *e.g.* state archives library should concentrate on regional histories and National Archives of India Library should be assigned the field of modern India history. Besides, modern Indian history, it can acquire publications of common interest to both. Under this programme, National Archives of India Library can acquire books and periodicals on archival sciences, preservation, reprography, etc. Besides, resource sharing on inter-library loan can play a significant role in tiding over the situation created by economic recession.

### 4. New Media in Collection Development : Technological Impact

The advent of new technology of collection development has revolutionised traditional methods of collection building. The emphasis is now more and more on procurement of publications in microforms. The archival libraries are no more exceptions to this change. They are now concentrating on oral history which are recorded on tapes after interviewing personalities related with the events.

### *4.1 Applications of Machines/Computers*

Computers are slowly replacing traditional methods of preparation of indexes in archives, which will ultimately result in non-acquisition of traditional form of book indexes. The archival libraries can now make effective use of computers in preparation of indexes, abstracts, etc.

### *4.2 Electronic Books and Journals*

Though the possibility of electronic books and journals forming part of archival collection is a remote possibility, but in future certainly they can form part of archival collection.

## 5. Collection-Building Processes, Users Participation

Archival libraries are already making optimum use of individuals/institutional user's participation in their collection building. It may be mentioned here that because of supply of number of publications on complimentary basis by the users of archival information, their collection-building processes are least hampered by economic recession.

### *5.1 Institutions and Organisations*

The archival libraries are receiving a number of publications issued by institutions and organisations free of cost for reference and record. These publications ultimately become part of our collection. Under IHRC resolutions 1972, National Archives of India Library is getting a number of publications published by governments, institutions and organisations. This phenomenon is peculiar in the sense that other special libraries do not enjoy this benefit of collection building.

### *5.2 Authors/Writers*

The users of records and publishers who have utilised archival information in writing their publications are required to deposit at least one copy of their publication for other users. By this way, they are helping archival libraries in their collection-building programmes.

### *5.3 Research Scholars*

The research scholars visiting archival libraries are its valuable clientele, who mostly come for research and reference on modern Indian history and regional histories of states. They contribute their might by depositing one copy of their research publications books to archival libraries under research rules. These publications also form part of our collection.

## 6. Conclusion

To enable the archival library to keep the adverse effect of economic recession on their collection development at its minimal level, these libraries must explore the possibility of co-operation and resource sharing through inter-library loan. If these policies and programmes are adopted by archival libraries it will enable them to meet the set goals of their organisations effectively; and also serve the user's interest best.

*Chapter 3*

# Information Retrieval in Archives and Archival Libraries in India: Models and Techniques

## 1. Introduction

The archives and records form an essential and significant part of nation's information resources and deal with information bearing materials generated within the administrative systems of the important organisations, while on the whole, library and documentation services deal with information bearing materials brought in from outside. To play this part, it is essential that the archives and the records services should operate efficiently within the limitations of available resources. Modern records and archives services have to deal with a vast amount of materials and have to find ways of exploiting their information contents under the constraints of a budget which is never generous. Those connected with dissemination of archival information must adopt to the changing circumstances created by widespread use of computers, and must identify and solve their problems in the light of experiences gained by other professionals.

## 2. Information Retrieval

Information Retrieval pertains to the finding of required information available in store of information or database. The view centres round the concept of selectivity which usually requires that a price to be paid in effort, time, money or in all the three. Informa-tion retrieval is a communication process by which authors or creators of record communicate with readers, but there is time lag in between creation of message or text and its delivery to the Information retrieval system user. The records of a database are created and assembled without any inkling of its exact readers and their use in differing circumstances. The computer system consisting of both hardware and software is known as Information Retrieval System which may include the database.

### 2.1 *Information Retrieval in Archives and Archival Libraries*

Choosing of models or selecting models for archives and archival libraries, criteria should be users' requirements which are presently being met by manual retrieval due to obvious reasons of resource crunch, etc. The holdings of archival libraries mostly comprise of primary sources, as such are of special interest to its clienteles. Current records of government agencies become semi-current or non-current depending on the frequency of their use in carrying out the activities of the institutions. Archives services can not overlook the inevitability with which different forms of automation are coming to dominate administrative methods. The advance of incoming technology may be delayed in some developing countries but its eventual coming is a foregone conclusion. Elsewhere in the world, the automation is being adopted very quickly. Therefore, information workers of developing countries as well have to face the technological challenge and must prepare themselves to learn to use automated systems, as these are becoming standard, discarding traditional systems. The automation is advantageous both in financial terms and in terms of change in the methods of work and attitudes of the staff. In fact, if the true costs of running manual operations are calculated and the true costs of the introducing electronic methods are compared with them, the changeover is usually not found to be necessarily very expensive. However, it is necessary to invest in new equipment, and this equipment needs infrastructure services and maintenance. The systems, which we intend to use must be planned carefully, and be well suited to the jobs which we desire to accomplish. It is needless to emphasize that automation will reduce the amount of routine work and increase the productivity of the staff. The constraints in introducing automation in archives may be attributed to paucity of resources and sometimes lack of appropriate expertise.

### *2.1.1 Models*

Users in many countries are now accustomed in getting their information by accessing computer systems online. Automatically constructed indexes or keyword retrieval has changed the approach by which users are guided towards relevant material. This aroused users expectations, thereby necessitating adoptation of new technical tools for handling of archival information. In the most advanced countries, network carrying bibliographical and archival information are already in daily use. We can follow their footprints at least to make a beginning by introducing online retrieval system. The usual approach in designing information services is to design the system most suited to the organisations' requirements. System designer always keeps in the mind the vary need of the clienteles of the organisation. The system which is most suitable to begin with is one, which allows random enquiries to be made to any concerning individual records and enables almost instant response to the queries. The key to the online processing is the provision of number of terminals connected to the processor. In online processing the terminals allow users to have access to individual records and update their contents, if necessary. However, the inherent problems in choosing appropriate model of information retrieval is that so far no study of users requirements and behaviours has been made by professional archivists.

### 2.1.2. *Commercial Packages which can be Adopted for Archival Description*

It is possible that many software packages designed for information retrieval can be adopted in an archival institution. However, success of adoption depends on the nature of task and the flexibility of the software. The selection of software has to be decided by the archivists keeping in view the operational aspect. Another criteria to be adopted while selecting the software is the cost of obtaining the package.

### 2.1.3. *Prospec & Prospec-SA*

The public record office in London has adopted a computer system known as *PROSPEC* which is a set of programmes for compiling finding aids based on the description and indexing of archives at the class level. The system extends into automated form for establishing administrative control over its holdings. Further, so for the inclusion of description of sub-classes is concerned, there is potentiality for developing the system. The same has been done in the *PROSPEC-SA* extension.

### 2.1.4 *Famulus*

It is bibliographical package which is being used in academic or research institutions since long. The package was meant for use in batch mode users and punched cards. Modern Records Centre at Warwick University, U.S.A., Rutherford Appleton Laboratory,

U.S.A., Northwest Sound Archives, and several Museums have been using this package. Liverpool University also employed it as a medium of training for student archivists. One of the advantages of this system is that the user may enter a data structure comprising named fields to its maximum, in some cases about 50 per record. However, it is relatively weak in the range of output formats which it will permit.

### 2.1.5 *Status*

This information retrieval package has made considerable progress among various archives offices. When we compare it with *FAMULUS,* this package seems to be more expensive. But its performance has been tried and tested in a number of institutions like British Antarctic Survey and British Architectural Library. It has demonstrated its potentiality to handle very large free text databases. It also facilitates searching as free text can be searched with Boolean logic in comparison to *FAMULUS*. Since it does not incorporate word processing facilities, its ability to produce custom design output is minimal. However, it is quite possible to introduce local software which can link work processor to input as well as output. The Southampton University application has produced database containing multi-level descriptions along with a catalogue of item descriptions based on seven-field record structure.

### 2.1.6 *Other Commercial Packages*

There are many other commercially available information retrieval packages including *CAIRS*, *ASSASSIN* and *STAIRS*. The *STAIRS* was experimented in the House of Lords Record Office, London for producing inventory of Acts of Parliament. An interesting feature of *STAIRS* is that although designed as software for use by large organisations, it has been developed for use with an electronic office communication systems known as *PROFS*. By using this system executives of organisations are not only to communicate with each other, but they can also have access to the main database. A few archival services have adopted database management software which is available for micro-computers. One such package is called dBase II and its improved version is known as dBase III which is compatible with most standard micro-computer. Pilkington Bros PLC uses it for the control of its record management system. Its archival adoption was experimented at the Hampshire Record Office, England for preparing an index of wills.

Likewise, another package is known as *DELTA* which was employed by the Dyfed Record Office, S.W. Wales (U.K.) with *ICLDRE* model 50 micro-computers, along with 10 Mb hard disks. The project was aimed at producing an inventory of records of charities operative in the countries' and is valuable for administrative reference as well as for research purpose. Peculiar feature of this programme is its letter writing facility. Archivists can make use of similar packages as and when these become easily available because these packages require little or no adoptation at all or front-end programming. The only disadvantage with this system is that they cannot provide for multi-purpose of central database management.

*2.1.7 In House Designed Software*

The availability of micro-computer at lower prices has motivated some archivists to go for writing their own softwares. The Computer Application Committee of the Society of Archivists demonstrated its potentiality at their annual conference held at London in 1984. The survey conducted by Bartle R. & Cook Michael examined the lively application of self-designed model at the South Humberside Area Record Office, London. In this model the Hardware was an intertec Superbrain DD (64 K RAM) having two disk drives and a centronic 737 printer. Other worth mentioning self-designed applications include the one at the West Sussex Record Office which uses a stock control system and yet another system designed by Leicestershire Museum Service & Record Office, England. The Special feature of this Leicestershire system is the key position of the MDA type input forms. These forms are not required to be filled manually and datas are entered inter-actively through formated screens. Screen prompts are used to guide the research queries.

The merits of an in-house automated systems can be put in three folds. First, the archives can procure an information system tailor-made to meet their local priorities. Second, when archivists can have access to the computer centre's equipment and personnel they need not bother about purchasing and updating their own equipment or about mastering computer programmes themselves. Third, the entry level costs particularly for major equipment and software can be reduced to a minimum. The in-house automation has been very successful at academic, business, governmental and museum archives. The institutions who have gone for this system are University of Illinois, University of South Africa, Illinois State Archives, DEERA & Co., and the Smith Sonian Institution. These and a few other repositories have found that their information storage and retrieval requirements can be met by working with their home institutions' central computing office to develop programmes and to get access to equipment.

## 2.2 *Special Systems*

Systems main aims are the realisation of communication processes known as information system. Human information processing systems, electronic data processing systems, and information retrievals systems are mechanisms specifically designed to enable the retrieval of information. The main concerns of information retrieval is the access to the intellectual content of information records. The information retrieval systems usually function within larger and more complex organisations. Hence, their design should be carefully planned in relation to the goals of the organisations. The systems available or applicable in other disciplines may not necessarily be suitable to archives. Therefore, we have to go for a system which has already been installed in archival institutions; and are being successfully operated.

## 3. Information Retrieval Languages

### *3.1 Natural Language*

Natural language is one which is naturally spoken and is in contrast with artificial languages such as Fortran which is designed and usually highly restrictive in vocabulary and syntax. Computers have been fairly successful, where the text is straight forward and explanatory in nature. This means selecting the words most appropriate to the subject or similar subject should be taken as pre-requisite. The ability of the computers to perform will certainly relieve users in retrieving desired information. In the context, it may be pertinent to point out that in manual retrieval of information, much of stored information is bound to be lost.

### *3.2 Artificial Language*

When the information to be represented is limited

in variability, it can be represented in highly compact and unambiguous form, cutting storage requirements and vastly simplifying the computer programmes that must interpret it. By user's training in the use of the language, the chance of usage errors can be minimised.

## 4. Information Retrieval Techniques

It is needless to mention that the creators of information resources have a relatively clear vision of what the materials are all about. The materials generated within the organisation should be more clearly understood by the providers of service than that of those from outside. There is a need to give more fillip to the information than that to the technology as such; and to recognise where the application of technology is suitable to the requirements of our organisation. This will help us in deciding how the cost of products and services is to be controlled. The goal must be to develop a sense of vision and mission in dealing with complicated issues of varying nature.

### *4.1 Search Strategy*

The objective of search strategy can usually be stated in terms of identifying the type of information desired and more so its quality, the reliability required, and the nascentness of the information, etc. It may here be pointed out that user's profile attempts to represent not only user's subject interest but also his search preferences as well as search pattern. Searching is done in selective dissemination of information system by the documentalist or information specialist who constructs the search profile by selecting a search term from thesaurus and other reference tools. However, the success of SDI system depends mainly on the construction of individual or group users profile. Therefore, we have to take utmost care on constructing the profile of administrators, decision makers, researchers, etc. The search strategy should ideally represent different degrees of intellectual efforts when compiling files and also should require different degrees of sophistication of computer facility. In the original query in the archives context, we can opt for search strategy *viz.* coordinate matching of terms without weights (C.T.) in which output is ranked in order of terms coordination level, *i.e.* in order of the number of matching profile and document terms. The selection is done keeping in view the requirements of the clienteles of archives information as most of our clients come for a particular document whose identity is known to them. Some of the basic difficulties which we are likely to encounter in search strategy may be: (i) scale (ii) multiple attributes (iii) variation of language and finally definability. In the context, it may be mentioned that there are three principal strategies being adopted by users (including staff users) to identify archival documents relevant to their enquiry. These are direct identification, browsing and scanning. Direct identification occurs when the user knows one or more of the identifying features of the documents sought. In browsing users read pages of the finding side in order to pick up any information or ideas which strike them as useful. However, in browsing, the users immediate retrieval objective often can not be stated. Free text descriptions such as those in the administrative/ custodial history or the content and character areas are most suitable fields for this strategy. While in scanning one is required to identify specific keywords, names, character strings or references by running the eye over the finding aid until these appear.

## 5. Text Retrieval

One of the tasks, either for the retrieval system or the search intermediary, is to examine the language used to describe needs, looking for the words and the pattern that should appear in the record. One of the great difficulties being experienced is that the information need could be expressed in words in many different ways in archives context. We have to go for a survey of users behaviour in this regard to ascertain most frequently used words by them for a subject. Text retrieval packages are designed specifically for text retrieval. Typically, the records are independent, of variable length and comprise mostly natural language texts. Primary access to it is through an inverted file of text terms which are drawn from the records as they are placed on the database. Access is by content, rather than structural position, although most systems provide some option for holding fixed format data. A particular feature of such software packages is the user related interfaces. These packages are used both to build in-house databases, and to support databases, available through the international and national online hosts.

### *5.1 Hypertext*

The hypertext can take many forms: a definition of a terms, an expansion of a summery, a discussion of a related topic, or an annotation. Footnotes are best example of a hypertext machanism in print, but the term usually is reserved for computerised systems. Hypertext and hypermedia depend on how will the author has established the various links.

### *5.2 Expert System*

Basically expert systems are software packages aims at providing expert consultancy advice and assistance aiming at problem solving in specialist fields of knowledge. The application of expert systems to the archives activities is yet to take off. The main drawback now in use of expert systems in archives is the limited knowledge domain that can be developed. For instance, an expert system can be created for a particular area of reference service, but it is not possible to create a knowledge to accommodate all aspects of reference service.

## 6. Automated Retrieval System

In view of the magniture and enormity of precious record holdings of NAI as well as various state Archives, the manual retrieval which is continuing, can not hold good for all the times to come as it can not cope up with the demand. The archival libraries were constrained to contend themselves with just manual retrieval of information mostly published by various government organisations. But the advent of computer has changed almost all the activities of the government. There is, therefore, no reason including insufficiency of funds to come in the way of switching over to the automation of IR. We need to adopt automated retrieval system as quickly as possible, so that the benefit of automation is not denied to the users of archives information. The system may also prove advantageous to decision makers and administrators who need instant information in their day-to-day decision-making processes.

### *6.1. Online Retrieval*

#### *6.1.1 The Development of IR Methodology*

Archives services can not ignore the inevitability with which different forms of automation are coming to dominate administrative methods. The advance of this new technology may be delayed in some developing countries, but it has eventually come to India. We, as information workers have to face a challenge; and must themselves learn to use automated systems, because these are becoming standard, replacing traditional systems. Though, going for automation is a costlier affair, but in fact if the true costs of running a manual operation are calculated, and the true costs of introducing electronic methods are compared with them, the changeover is usually not found to be necessarily very expensive. Online retrieval allows random enquiries to be made to any concerning individual records and enables almost instant response to the queries. Fundamental to online processing is the provision of number of terminals connected to the processor. These terminals are usually either a key board and VDU combination of type-writer and printer. Terminals, connected to the processor locally by telephone line, allow different departments to have direct access to files held by the control processor. Databases can also be interrogated locally or remotely by different kinds of users.

## 7. Evaluation in IR Systems

In evaluating retrieval system or an information service one monitors and assesses its operation and performance, whether it is suitable to continue and whether it can be improved. The evaluation is also necessary to relate the present achievement to the goals and objectives of the organisation. Our ability to assess the return of our investment provides us the opportunity to choose between alternatives in the design, implementation or even in operational phases of the development of an IRS. Evaluation also helps us to know where the system stands and what remedy could be taken if it does not provide desired results.

## 8. Cost Benefit Considerations of IRS

### *8.1 Cost*

We cannot overlook cost while planning automated systems. In the very first step of policy formulation we need to have at least a broad idea of the costs of attaining certain goals. While taking decision, we shall need to draw the best estimate we can of the likely net gain or loss to the archives service from the courses of our action, we are considering. The next stage of cost benefit analysis comes when we monitor the success of the project.

### *8.2 Benefit*

The most obvious benefit being derived from the computer system wherever installed, has been for the staff who have been able to improve their performances. The same old staff on the stationery cost were able to produce more lists because of the application of the computer. As far as effectiveness is concerned, we shall need to concentrate on the costs of retrieving information from our systems. What is the costs of finding the information we need from the present system? What is the cost to the user of not finding all the relevant information because of the limitations of the old finding aids? What is the cost of staff-time in trying to help track down items that have not yet been properly listed? How do these compare to the costs of the computer-based system? The automated system can reduce the distasteful work and promote clear vision to the benefit of staff and ultimately of users. Alternatively a poor system can waste time, lower morals and induce counter-productive fear. A well designed system will give benefits but the savings will be enjoyed by our successors who will take for granted the freedom and flexibility the system gives them.

## 9. Conclusion

The ultimate aim of every models and techniques of IR is to provide quick information to the user, as traditional archival information services cannot cope up with the situation, therefore, these are required to be replaced by modern techniques of dissemination of information. Modernisation implies the advent of sophisticated techniques to control information and application of automated information methods for the dissemination of archival information. It is needless to mention that archives and record services cannot ignore the inevitability with which various forms of automation are coming to dominate administrative systems, as such, the incoming of new technology though a little bit delayed but has eventually come to India. The fear that the automation is very expensive one, is exaggerated. In fact, if the true costs of running a manual operations are calculated, and the true costs of introducing electronic methods are compared with them, the changeover is usually not found to be necessarily very expensive one.

*Chapter 4*

# Networking of Archives and Archival Libraries: Problems and Prospects

## 1. Introduction

The archives and record form an essential and significant part of nation's information resources and deal with information bearing materials generated within the administrative systems of the important organisations, while on the whole, library and documentation services deal with information bearing materials brought in from outside. To play this part, it is essential that the archives and the record services should operate efficiently within the limitations of available resources. Modern records and archives services have to deal with a vast amount of materials and have to find ways of exploiting their information contents under the constraints of a budget which is never generous. Those connected with dissemination of archival information must adapt to the changing circumstances created by widespread use of computers, and must identify and solve their problems, in the light of experiences gained by other professionals.

However, there are a number of inter-related factors which are working against the application of computers in Indian Archival Institutions. First, the country lacks 'computer literacy' which is necessary in appreciating the positive aspect of computerisation. Second, there has not been enough financial support from funding agencies for archives to go in for computerisation. Third, archivists in India did not have adequate knowledge in the theoretical and practical aspects of archival computerisation to enable them to take up the project of networking. But, during the 1990's, there has been growing enthusiasm in favour of archives computerisation. It is, therefore, expected that computerisation of archives and information operations and services will become an accepted policy before the nation enters the 21st century.

## 2. Planning and Designing of Archives and Archival Libraries Networking in India

User in many countries are now accustomed in getting their information by accessing computer systems online. In the most advanced countries, network carrying bibliographical and archival information are already in daily use. We can follow their footprints at least to make a beginning by introducing online retrieval system. The usual approach in designing information services is to design the system most suited to the organisations requirements. Probably, the most difficult task of introducing automation is deciding on and writing the initial system specification. This has to be done before experience in running any automated system has been gained, so the archivists or record managers have to confront with a difficult task. They have to analyse the work of their service, and set out clearly which processes are to be considered for automation and to match these against the capabilities of the system. Yet, the best way of assessing system capabilities can be done by gaining good experience. For this reason, it may be desirable to send archivists or records managers to observe or get help of automated system of another matching service, just to acquire some basic experience. For the purpose, the staff of the archives or records service must be regarded as an essential resource. Among these categories, we can include managerial, professional and supporting staff. It is also essential that all these people must receive appropriate training and be willing to actively participate in the automated system to make it a success.

At the outset, two approaches are possible. One is to consider the introduction of a total automated system, covering all or many of the main functions of the archives service in an integrated way. The other is to think of introducing a limited system to carry out just one function in a specialist manner. Although, the potential of the first is likely to be realised eventually, only a few archives services have gone for it. As far as the second approach is concerned, it is more fruitful and being successfully applied in a number of archival institutions.

However, computer systems are not always a good answer in achieving organisational goals. Sometime they introduce inflexibilities unnessarily complex methods, or antegonize the staff so such that the end is worse than the beginning.

Costs will be a significant feature, and comparison of cost in between automated and manual methods is required to be done. If a computer system does survive the test, it should be adopted without any hesitation. Further, there are certain infrastructural requirements which must be met before considering automation. It is utmost essential that there should be uninterrupted supply of electricity which is usually not available in developing countries. Another infrastructural question is setting of work stations where the processing of data is to be done. The first internal collection of data about archives usually occurs in the work room, where the material is being sorted out.

### *3.1 Commercial Packages which can be Adopted for Archival Description*

It is possible that many software packages

designed for information retrieval can be adopted for works within an archives. However, success of adoption depends on the nature of task and the flexibility of the software. The selection of software is decided by the archivists depending on the operations. Another criteria in selection is the cost of obtaining the package.

### *3.1.1 Prospec & Prospec-SA*

The Public Record Office in London has adopted a computer system known as *PROSPEC* which is a set of programmes for compiling finding aids based on the description and indexing of archives at the class level. The system extends into automated form for establishing administrative control over its holdings. Further, there is potentiality for developing the system, as regards inclusion of description of sub-classes are concerned. The same has been done in the *PROSPEC-SA* extension.

### *3.1.2 FAMULUS*

It is a bibliographical package which is being used in academic or research institutions since long. The package was meant for use in bach mode users, punched cards. Besides Modern Record Centre, Warwick University, U.S.A. at the Rutherford Appleton Laboratory, U.S.A. and at the Northwest Sound Archives, Several Museums also make use of it.

Liverpool University also employed it as a medium for training of student archivists. It has a number of advantages. One such advantage is that the user may enter a data structure comprising named fields to its maximum, in some cases about 50 per record. However, it is relatively weak in the range of output formats which it will permit.

### *3.1.3 Status*

This information retrieval package has made considerable progress among various archives offices. When we compare it with *FAMULUS* this package seems to be expensive to procure, but its performance has been tried and tested in a number of institutions. These include BAS (British Antarctic Survey) and the British Architectural Library. Further, it has demonstrated its potentiality to handle very large free text databases. This package facilitates searching as free text can be searched with Boolean logic in comparison to *FAMULUS*. It does not incorporate word processing facilities, consequently, its ability to produce custom design output is minimal. However, it is quite possible to introduce local software which can link word processor to input & output both. The Southampton University application has produced database containing multi-level descriptions along with a catalogue of item descriptions based on seven-field record structure.

### *3.1.4 Other Commercial Packages*

There are many other commercially available

information retrieval packages including *CAIRS*, *ASSASSIN* and *STAIRS*. The *STAIRS* was experimented by the House of Lords Record Office, London for producing inventory of Acts of Parliament. But financial problems halted the project '*STAIRS*'. Other interesting feature of STAIRS is that although designed as software for use by large organisations, it has been developed for use with an electronic office communication systems known as *PROFS*. The system enables executive of organisations not only to communicate with each other, but they can also have access to the main database. This is the peculiar facility which organisations can expect in the near future. A few archival services have adopted database management software which is available for microcomputers. One such package is called dBase II and its improved version is known as d Base III which is compatible with most standard makes of microcomputer. Pilkington Bros PLC uses it for the control of its record management system. Its archival adoptation was experimented at the Hempshire Record Office, England for creating an index of wills.

Another likewise package is known as *DELTA* which was employed by the Dyfed Record Office, S.W. Wales (U.K.) with ICL DRS model 50 microcomputers, with 10 Mb hard disks. The project was aimed at producing an inventory of records of charities operative in the countries and is valuable for administrative reference as well as for research.

Peculiar feature of this programme is its letter writing facility. Archivists can make use of similar packages as and when these become easily available as they require little or no adoptation at all or front-end programming. But they have some demerits as they can not provide for multipurpose or central database management.

### *3.2 In-house Designed Software*

The availability of micro-computer at lower prices has motivated some archivists to go for writing their own softwares. The computer application committee of the Society of Archivists demonstrated its potentiality at their annual conference of 1984. The survey conducted by Bartle, R & Cook, Michael examined the lively application at the South Humberside Area Record Office. The hardware was an intertec Superbrain DD (64 K RAM) having two disk drives and a centronic 737 printer. Other worth mentioning self-designed applications include work at the West Sussex Record Office which uses a stock control system and also system designated by Leicestershire Museum Service & Record Office, England. The special feature of this Leicestershire system is the key position of the MDA type input forms. These forms are not required to be filled manually; data are entered interactively through formated screens. Screen prompts are used to guide the research queries.

The merits of an in-house automated system can

be put in three folds. First, the archives can procure an information system tailor-made to meet their local priorities. Second, when archivist can have access to the computer centre's equipment and personnel need not bother about purchasing and updating their own equipment or about mastering computer programmes themselves. Third, the entry level costs particularly for major equipment and software, can be reduced to a minimum. The in-house automation has been very successful at academic, business, governmental and museum archives. The institutions who have gone for this system are University of Illinois, University of South Africa, Illinois State Archives, Deera & Co., and the Smith Sonian Institution. These and a few other repositories have found that their information storage and retrieval requirements can be met by working with their home institutions 'Central Computing Office' to develop programmes and to get access to equipment.

For in-house systems a very careful advance planning is required to ensure that whatever system is adopted will ultimately serve the users of archives and archivists alike. Like any other decision, the choice of automated information system should also be based on study of its feasibility. One is required to go ahead only if the study reveals enough need, adequate funds, and a good institutional base.

## 4. Management of Archival Network

Cost effective strategies should form part of system management. There is no point in running any service unless it is found to be useful; there must be an adequate return for the money invested. This is true of manual systems just as much as for automated ones. In the Indian situation, we have to keep in mind that the transition from manual to automated system has to be smoothly organised. Due care needs to be taken for generating trained manpower, arranging training facilities for creating each network. Some kind of mechanism should also be evolved to regularly test the efficiency of the system, and for checking that its output really corresponds to the needs of user clientele. General system should carry a potentiality for the radical alteration of the product. So for it has been assumed that computers are an alternative way of executing what has been effected in the past by manual methods; the establishment of administrative control over archival processes, and production of traditionally defined finding aids like guides or inventories. But if used to the full, computers could be finding aids of quite a new kind. From a single database consisting of archival descriptions of one or more repositories, it could produce an indefinite number of selected lists in different orders.

Archivists are not adopting computers for the management of their own organisations. It is probably not common for an archives service to be administratively responsible for its own financing and personnel management as these services are usually being done by the employing agency. The Public Archives of Canada has a system for automated office applications and administrative systems covering financial, personnel and inventory control.

## 5. Implementation of Archives Networks

It is very difficult to fix a period for changeover from manual to automated one. The correct way is for the new system to be allowed to run in parallel with the old (manual) one for a trial period; and during this period the drawbacks and 'bugs' of the new one need to be identified and properly dealt with. The affected staff should be taken into confidence at every level. This is important because the hostility of staff members, however, unreasonable it may seem, may cause failure of the new system. The computer system should help people to perform more effectively in congenial atmosphere. If the administration fails to convince the staff about the merits of the system, it would perhaps be better not to introduce the change. There are a number of systems in the field of archives which are in operation at present, but they are not standard one. As such, any new venture still has potentiality of repercussions in the archives world. It is, therefore, expected from those who are considering introduction of computer systems in any way should bring the facts in the notice of their co-professionals;

and allow inspection soon after implementation. The discussion and opinion of other professionals at the planning stage will certainly prove beneficial.

Implicit in projects for multi-repository guides is the possibility of a network: a system in which the finding aids of a number of linked repositories are made available by automated means. Such systems have long been available for bibliographical or scientific materials on both national and international levels. Archivists have been slow to develop this aspect of their work, not only because of the inherent difficulty of standardising unique and varied materials but also because the need for very rapid access at remote sites was less easy to demonstrate in their case. However, a number of online network are now in use. The most highly organised one is to be found in USA known as *SPINDEX* users network which uses software package developed in the Library of Congress and at the National Archives.

## 6. International Computerised Networks: Their Relevance to Archival Networks in India

There are a number of international online networks, the most organised among them are to be found in USA, which is known as *SPINDEX* users' network developed during 1970's. This network uses a software package developed in the Library of Congress and at the National Archives. This has since been replaced by two library-based networks known as RLIN and OCLC. There are a few more networks which are using software available through library or museum sources, or utilizing business stock control packages. The BAS (British Antarctic Survey) has adopted cataloguing card designed by the Museum Documentation Association as input data forms enabling it to use two different software packages on the same data.

The BAS approach is simple one and can be adopted even in smaller archival services. However, there are problems with regards to the levels of description, but these can be overcome by using cards for group and series level descriptions, as well as for item descriptions. In view of the simplicity of BAS, it can be easily emulated in National Archives as well as in various State Archives as and when decision is taken to start a network in between National Archives and States Archives.

In Indian archival information services work; the computer can be applied in two ways. First, it can be utilised to build up an in-house storage and retrieval system which is limited to the resources available in archival institutions and give information services to its clientele. Secondly, the computer can be used as an access tool to obtain information from externally operated information storage and retrieval systems. The in-house or local information retrieval system can be designed to cater to the requirements of users of an archival institution based on its archival resources.

## 7. Future Perspective of Indian Archival Networks

We notice that the environment for archives networks in India is picking up. India can not afford to spend a large sums on developing networks like RLIN (Research Libraries Information Network) and OCLC (Ohio College Library Consortium), although it is important, but it can and should afford development of archives network like BAS in the National Archives and various State Archives to begin with. The question before the Indian archivists is that of the cost which is most crucial factor whether or not to replace manual system by automated system. It is quite clear that extra costs will be involved but it is not known whether these extra costs will buy extra productivity and means of access. Most of the archivists where automation has been introduced are of the opinion that automation is advantageous both in financial terms and in terms of change in the methods of work and attitudes of the staff. In fact, if the true costs of running a manual operation are calculated and the true costs of introducing electronic methods are compared with them, the changeover is usually not found to be necessarily very expensive. It may be useful for Indian archivists to draw some lessons from the experiences of archivists of countries like U.K. and USA.

## 8. Conclusion

The ultimate aim of every network is to provide quick information to the user. As traditional manual archival information services can not cope up with the situation, therefore, these are required to be replaced by modern techniques of dissemination of information. Modernisation implies the advent of sophisticated techniques to control information and application of automated information methods for the dissemination of archival information. It is needless to emphasise that archives and record services cannot ignore for a longer period the inevitability with which various forms of automation are coming to dominate administrative systems. The incoming of new technology may be delayed in India, but its eventual coming is very much certain. The fear that the automation is very expensive one, is exaggerated. In fact, if the true costs of running a manual operation are calculated, and the true costs of introducing automation are compared with them, the changeover is usually not found to be necessarily very expensive one. It is, therefore, suggested that the manual retrieval of information in Archives is required to be phased out to enable Indian archival institutions to cope up with increased volume of information to the utmost benefit of its clientele.

*Chapter 5*

# Archive Library Relations

## 1. Introduction

One of the peculiar characteristic of human being is his desire to communicate with his fellow beings. This resulted in creation of recorded knowledge. Since very dawn of the civilization the societies took pains to store and preserve this recorded knowledge at safest places so that this could be utilised by present as well as future generations. The outcome was creation of libraries followed by archives. Documents were carefully preserved in libraries since the very origin of writing. There is no doubt that these were meant to be consulted occasionally by lot of privileged persons and, therefore, were accessible only to a few. The archives were first opened to the historians by some European countries from 18th century. But to our surprise, in some countries, even today scientific or academic researchers are the privileged one who have access to archives; and general public is usually discouraged to use archival materials. However, there are no such restriction in case of use of library materials. Archives and libraries both are the repositories for the records of human culture. These records exhibit the scholarly and creative efforts of a civilizations and also social and historical interaction. These are truely a gift from past generations to the future generations. We have, therefore, the solemn duty to preserve these records to discharge our responsibility, which has been bestowed on our shoulders. Modern society is much more dependent on research and information than ever before. It is because much information is required, produced and consumed in developed countries, therefore, the concept of "information exploration" has become a hard reality, not only for the librarians and information scientists, but to the archivists as well. The mass production of information has become of equal concern to both the archivists and librarians as far as its management aspect is concerned.

### 1. 1 History

Ever since evolution of writing, archives have since then been serving rulers of the nations. Whether recorded on stone or clay tablets, on the papyri or palm strips, on parchment or papers, archives have always been carefully preserved under protection of someone depending on their quantity and on existing facilities. However, it was the French Revolution which necessitated the enactment of Archives Act of 1794; and thereby launched a new era in the history of archives. But research condition in archives remained inconducive to researchers because of strict enforcement of regulations governing the use, which continued up to the end of second world war. Until the mid 15th century, records were not distinguished from library materials and were taken care of by the librarians like other manuscripts preserved in the libraries. The importance given nowadays to public records is direct consequence of the French Revolution, resulting in an independent national system of archives administration. From its very beginning, UNESCO has supported efforts which were aimed at gradual elimination of restriction and the increased liberalization relating to access to archives. The Dutch archivist, Dr. F.R.J. Verhoeven, recently appropriately characterized the role of a modern policy of access to archives stressing that '. . . making the archives of national and historical value available to the people is a moral obligation of any democratic government and for that reason national archives have also been called the ultimate conscience of the Government. As regards use of library materials are concerned, Dr. S.R. Ranganathan all along has been a protagonist of open access in the libraries. His continued struggle in this direction compelled a number of university libraries in India to allow open access to their collection to facilitate maximum use.

## 2. Buildings

For archives and libraries, control of environmental conditions are of utmost concern which are dependent with the types of buildings in which these were housed. The building used for this purpose is, therefore, required to be maintained properly and should be free from problems like condensation, oxidisation of metallic parts, etc. to ensure suitable storage condition for documents. Although, a few archives and libraries buildings have been built keeping in view the requirements, but a number of buildings were not constructed for such purposes. In a number of cases, archives and libraries are still utilizing old buildings not constructed for this purpose. These buildings are, therefore, often over-crowded and lack proper maintenance like leaking of roofs, improperly fitted windows, doors, cracked pipes, etc. There is, therefore, utmost need to improve conditions of such buildings being utilised for housing archives and libraries. It has been noticed that more libraries were housed in buildings constructed for the purpose in comparison to archives. Mr. E. Ketelaar suggests that at the time of accepting a fresh proposal to build new archival premises or to alter existing one, the plans should be made available for the scrutiny to the archival authority before adapting them. The opinion of the archival authority should also invariably be sought before taking premises on hire for archival purposes. In case, where new buildings are being planned, requirements for security and fire control should also be incorporated into the structure of the building meant to be utilised for archives and libraries.

### 3. Accessibility

Libraries are collecting agencies and usually select the material from wide ranging existing choices in accordance with the predetermined acquisition policy, which can, however, need to be adjusted in changing circumstances. Acquisitions are usually done by purchase or gift. In today's information society, right to access to information is recognised as individuals birth right. In many countries, freedom to access to information and privacy laws go side by side ensuring individual's access to information; and at the same time privacy in case of private papers. The open access in most of the libraries of the world has since come to stay. But the archival institutions had rarely allowed open access as in their view, it implies risk of loss. Libraries of printed books can, however, afford that very loss as use is their main objective. In the case of archival materials, authorities seems to be well-justified in not allowing open access as usually only one copy of each document is available in their repository. Public archives, by their very nature, are part and parcel of the governmental and administrative framework of a country. Hence, it is quite logical if one demands that they may be opened without any restriction for the purpose of research. But, by demanding that they should be accessible to each and every researcher, one should keep in mind that their very existence is not endangered as they are part and parcel of the heritage of each and every country. Mr. Dazie rightly remarked at the extraordinary International Congress on Archives held at Washington in 1966 on the subject of 'the opening of archives to research': "in the developing countries, libralisation of access to archives must begin with their safeguarding and organisation." Undoubtedly the most vital service which archivist can render to a researcher is to provide access to the material desired by him/her. However, certain materials can be restricted to safeguard national security or personal privacy. But, archivist should endeavour/strive to make available to the researchers as much material as possible. However, there is no reason to deny the fact that ultimate aim of archives like libraries is use of the documents in its holding/custody as their motto is also that user must be able to retrieve the document easily.

## 4. Collections

### *4.1 Archives and Library Materials*

The most important basic material which comprise of the library collections is still the paper—a material composed of cellulose. But, in the last few years, the reproduction of recorded knowledge is coming more and more on to polymer materials, called microforms, which is playing a revolutionary role in supplementing the classical form of paper. On the other hand, archival materials still comprise of single sheet materials, *viz.* files, maps, plans, charts, volumes, textiles, photographs, audio–visual machine readable records, etc. The reading materials in the library are mostly in printed form. On the other hand, the materials kept in an archives mostly comprise of manuscripts. However, there are certain exception as well as there are a few printed forms appended to the manuscripts. These are unique and integral part of the manuscripts.

### *4.2. Photographs and Photographic Materials*

Photographs and photographic materials since their very inception have been of common concern to both archives and libraries. In addition to very use of photographs by archives and libraries, its role and importance is also noticed by their use in exhibitions and publications containing photographs; and also their more and more use by authors and researchers. No doubt, paper had been the predominent document materials in archives and libraries through centuries but, now-a-days, it is steadily being replaced by photographic materials like microfilms, microfiches, etc. Another use of photographic records is equally made in motion picture films which can be used in documentary form in order to record historical events or as a medium of artistic expression. Anyone or all of these major application of photographic records is being made in libraries and archives. However, in a number of archives and libraries photographic equipments and processing facilities are being channelised for different purposes other than for which the unit was meant for. In this regard, a survey jointly undertaken by IFLA and ICA published in 1987 points out that a large number of archives and libraries claim to have a photographic unit in their institutions, but only half of these expressed satisfaction with their exis-ting equipment. Moreover, 36 per cent of archives and 43 per cent of libraries were found to diversi-fying processing facilities for different purposes.

### *4.3 Microfilm and Microfiche*

The important basic material of the library collection still remains the paper which is composed more or less of cellulose. But in the last few years, the reproduction of recorded knowledge on to polymer materials known as microforms has increasingly spread both in archives and libraries and going to supplement the classical form of paper. The very in-coming of new technology in the later 20th century has revolutionised both the creation of original material in audio–visual and machine readable form; and its more and more adoption by archives and libraries. Now, microfilm, microfiche, gramophone records, film and magnetic tapes are all found in reading rooms of both either as copies of original or substitution copies meant for use by researchers.

## 4.4 Collection Development Policies

While formulating collection development policies, the need of various types of clienteles must be taken into account. Foremost among them are the decision makers whose requirements need to be given due importance. Decision makers often need information, which is usually available in records and archives. To them, library materials are next in importance as these are secondary sources of information. As regards holdings of libraries and archives are concerned, archivists and librarians have similar objective *i.e.* to make these available efficiently and at the minimum possible cost, if any. To meet this objective, both should know in general what information they can provide to users from their own collections. To achieve this end, the archivist should also explore the possibility of providing information from the treasures of published reference works which is the domain of librarians. Similarly, the librarian should also see to it that what kind of information can be located in unpublished manuscripts and archives owned by them.

## 4.5 Acquisition Policy

The methods and procedures followed by librarians for organising materials and services were more uniform than those practiced by archives. But this phenomenon was occurring because of the differing nature of publications and archival documents. The archival documents originated from various organisations, and as such are invariably in various fonds, groups, series and classes which does not hold good in case of published materials acquired by libraries. It was, therefore, quite easier for librarians to formulate techniques for acquiring publications and to get it further developed and revised based on personal experiences. Though, archivists are acquisitive by nature, and in the past, they were the persons who were responsible for centralising most of the valuable records in repositories, however, there is still enough scope for improvement in their acquisition policies as the researchers are required to be served on the pattern of services offered by the libraries and information centres. The librarians are well aware of acquisition problems, and, as such, made sincere efforts to balance the cost of purchase, processing, etc. Many archival institutions were unable to formulate appropriate acquisition policies as they do not have enough budget for the purpose. Unlike libraries, they are handicapped in the sense that they cannot visualize identical materials elsewhere other than their usual domain.

### *4.6 Appraisal of Materials*

In libraries, the selection of publications is done in accordance with a set of principles keeping in view the requirements of the clienteles of the institutions/ organisation to whom the library is to cater. But as for as appraisal of records, it is quite impossible to create a likewise yardstick for selection of records. At the most, the archivist can formulate principles for appraising records, and these principles can serve as guidelines to achieve the purpose. No doubt, the most important professional activity of the archivists is record appraisal, which is very difficult task to perform. This is mainly because once a decision is taken for the destruction of records, it cannot be undone and the information contained in those records may not be obtainable from other sources. The person/archivist performing this duty is supposed to be capable of understanding the nature and trend of research and is also required to have requisite knowledge of the history of that country. His familiarity with other materials useful for research in the archives, in libraries, in documentation centres, etc. will prove to be of added advantage to the institutions/organisations in catering to the requirement of modern research. The fundamental approach followed by archivists and librarians while selecting the materials to be kept in archives/libraries differ in the sense that while evaluating materials produced by governmental or private bodies, the archivist. He, therefore, normally selects records for retention in the aggregates, not as a single item. He, further, selects them keeping in view the functions of the organisation rather than subject as is being done by the librarian. The role of archivist is also unique in the sense that his judgements are final and irrevocable because the records once destroy can not be retrieved. Contrary to approach of archivists, librarian evaluates the materials for acquisition as a single item. However, the right judgement of the librarian depends on his/her having a sound knowledge of principles and techniques of library science, current trend in modern research and his familiarity with the requirements of researchers and administrators.

### 4.7 *Selection of Materials*

Library materials are certainly meant to be utilized, while archival materials are also preserved for consultations. But, archives usually retain permanently each and every material which they collect in their day-to-day transactions. Both have many similarities as far as users needs are concerned. However, there are some typical problems which are to a large extent relate to archives only. Archives are created organically by individuals and institutions in the course of their day-to-day transactions primarily for their own use and are not meant for use and information of others, whereas published materials housed in the libraries are for the utilization of its users. What librarians often term "Government Documents," i.e. printed reports of departments, is in fact, selection from archival materials for information of the public at large through their publication programme. However, after being published these materials become part and parcel of library materials. Library materials are certainly meant to be used, while archival materials are also preserved for consultation. The archives are concerned to retain permanently everything which comes to their possession after appraisal. Archive and library materials both are kept primarily for the purpose of consultation, but libraries are frequented by general public as well as those having special subject interests resulting in heavier use of library materials, which is not true in case of archives materials. The ordinary collection of books, etc. is the result of selection by library personnel keeping in view the requirements of their clienteles. On the contrary, archives is a single organisation which has not been made, but has grown for reasons and circumstances quite different for the interests, which utilises its printed materials coming under the perview of librarians, but in certain cases, they may acquire archival materials *e.g.* newspapers received by governments in consequence of its activity or circulars enclosed with government documents become part of archives. Audio-visual and cartographic materials are of common concern to archivists as well as librarians. Sir Hilary Jenkinson opines that archives are not collected as they came together and reached their final arrangements by a natural process or a growth. On the other hand, librarians do not derive their materials from particular bodies. They are obtaining these from the sources best known to them. Prior to the archivists being recognised as profession, librarians were custodian of archives. Certain archival institutions had their beginning made in manuscripts division of libraries. The Library of Congress, *e.g.* was custodian of archives of Federal Government before the National Archives came into existence.

### *4.8 Accessioning*

The main function of an archives accession register is to record and preserve permanently group of archives received on transfer, etc. This register can also be utilised to carry out other functions and as such, may serve as a starting point for an effective administrative control. The data can also be utilised to provide a receipt for transferring body or originator; and may serve as a check list for the compilation of administrative task and processes within the service. In the archives context, the accessioning is the act and procedure involved in a transfer of legal title and taking of records or papers into the physical custody of an archival agency, records centres or manuscript repository. On the other hand, library accession register is a record of publications added to the library collection in the order of their acquisitions. For each publication, the accession register gives its bibliographical identification, source, cost, and accession number, etc.

### *4.9 Classification and Cataloguing*

The unique and unfamiliar nature of contents of

archives would require their arrangements even more necessitating than that of publications in the libraries. The arrangements of entries can make or mark the usefulness of the catalogue. In other words, efficiency of archival service would also depend equally on correct and depth classification, which is much more imperative than that of the efficiency of library and information service. Like library classification, the similar technique be applied for archival classification as well as and when the decision is taken to classify archival documents subjectwise. Further time/period sequences is equally important like subject order in archival classification. However, information contained in each record varies, therefore, it will certainly put a severe strain on the notation of archival classification. The difference in methods and approach in the library and archival profession is also reflected in the arrangement of their materials. While the term classification is used in both the professions, its connotation is not the same. When it is applied to archives, it means their arrangements within an archival organisation according to their provenance and in relation to the organisation and functions of the creating agencies. However, if classification is in relation to library materials, it means grouping items in accordance with a predetermined logical scheme of arrangements by providing notations. However, archivists are handicapped in this regards as they cannot arrange their materials in accordance with a predetermined scheme of subject "classification". Another difference noticed in between archives and library professions relate to descriptions. The term "cataloguing" is also used in both the professions, again having different meanings like that of classification. Library cataloguing is usually applicable to publications only. On the other hand, if its materials are at all catalogued in archives, the same is done unitwise which are aggregates of items, *e.g.* groups or series. In view of the foregoing analysis, it is apparent that the basic methodological differences between these two professions arise mainly because of the nature of the materials at their disposal.

### *4.10 Indexing*

Index language is a vocabulary of terms used to represent the subject matter. Such vocabulary can be divided into (*a*) control vocabularies; and (*b*) natural language. Librarians has since long been using common vocabularies, which included tools such as Dewey Decimal Classification, U.D.C. or the Library of Congress Classification, etc. for arranging their publications as well as standard list of subject headings. In archives, the location of each record is computed through the use of an index. The key words are contained in a separate index which can be rapidly searched to know, if particular record is available, and if so, their location. The technique adopted by librarians in developing and standardizing subject headings list may be certainly of help to archivist in preparation of their finding aids, if the need is felt to reorganise the records subjectwise; and also in the selection of terms to be used in preparing a subject index for an archival finding aid, *viz.* guide, inventory or special list.

## 4.11 Preservation and Conservation

Archivists, librarians, curators, and conservators have all a common shared professional duty to ensure that items of their collections are maintained in a condition appropriate to their use. It is, therefore, utmost essential for those responsible for maintenance and upkeeping of archives and libraries to formulate a policy of their own in respect of preservation of their respective collections to fulfil the aims and objectives of their organisations. Preservation policy for both archives and libraries should aim at ensuring best possible condition for storage, use, and exhibition of materials. However, financial resources, accommodation and climate will certainly have some bearing on the formulation of preservation policy. Archivists and librarians are now realising the very fact of good investment in climate control, control of light, good storage, fire protection and security of their materials from theft and vandalism with the hope that it will certainly yield dividend in near future. However, state of preservation/ conservation differs in each and every archives and libraries. In this regard, a survey of state of conservation in archives and libraries conducted jointly by IFLA and ICA shows that archives were provided with better conservation facilities in comparison to libraries. In libraries, good maintenance practices were noticed. Archives undertook fumigation of their collections more frequently, concentrated more on control of environment in view of uniqueness of their holdings. On the other hand, libraries were just concentrating on cleaning, furbishing and boxing. Out of 58 per cent countries surveyed, only 16 were found to be having a national preservation policy. In the context, it may be emphasised that care of collection is equally important as acquisition and organisation of materials. Therefore, archives and libraries should strike for making adequate budgetary provisions for the purpose. With good planning, one can ensure environmental modification which will enable institutions to reduce chances of damage by mould to their collection. In this regard, archivists and librarians share a common conviction that the mould must be killed. Beside this, archives and libraries community is equally concerned with insects, and other pests which are common enemies for both library and archival materials for a number of reasons. First and foremost among these are the commitment of both to preserve the collection for future use. Insects and mould can reduce the printed words to excrement; obliterate page after page and cause fungal destruction; destroy binding covers and valuable documents. The second concern is the economic loss caused by these insects and mould. A third consideration is the psychological revulsion of the staff and public to pests which they think comes in their way of facility to utilize the materials. The last, but not least is the concern of various health and sanitation agencies as they think that it is their obligation to ensure public health from transmission of diseases.

## 5. Services to Clienteles

### *5.1 Users' Service*

The archivist owe much obligations to their clienteles because of the uniqueness of their holdings in comparison to librarians who are only required to provide information contained in the publications. However, care required for consultation by users of public records is to be much more than that of printed publications housed in the libraries. The records need gentler handling as these are usually old being prone to perishing if handled recklessly. It is, therefore, required from every user to leave the records after consultations as far as possible in the same condition in which they were got issued. The rules of archives are restrictive in contrast to the rules of libraries, which are framed to promote best use of publications. Every publication acquired by the library must be related to its users' requirements. A library is, therefore, also like an archives, or a repository in which society finds what it has accumulated through centuries. In todays world, archivists and librarians alike are concerned and are swimming for their lives in a sea of symbols, and technology is only of limited help to them to fulfil their expectations because of newer and newer innovation in the field of information transfer. Archives usually pass through three phases while providing information to their potential users. In the first phase, there are current files which may be required at any time for reference. In the second phase, the files may be desired on certain occasions for the purpose of precedent and also for historical background in connection with official work. Finally, these are authentic and valuable primary source material for the purpose of research. To cater to the needs of their clients, archivists and librarians will benefit immensely from each other's experiences. In this regard, librarians can study archivists' method of content description, and archivists can benefit by studying preparation of standard formats, indexing and thesaurus construction to which librarians and information scientists have given particular attention.

### 5.2 *Documentation Service*

An unique relationship exists in between archives and libraries which is their shared aim to acquire, preserve and make information readily available in the form of documentation. The very origins, character and use of archival information, however, require the application of different principles and techniques which is applicable to published information in the custody of libraries. In archives context, documentation is meant organisation and processing of documents or data which includes location, identification, acquisition, analysis, storage, retrieval, presentation and circulation for the information of users. This is quite distinct and different from the meaning of documentation from librarian's point of view, an inkling of which is available from the very definition of Association of Special Libraries and Information Bureaus (U.K.) which says that it is "recording, organisation and dissemination of specialised knowledge".

## *5.3 Abstracting Service*

In the modern library system, no library can discharge its obligation to users unless it provides abstracting services keeping in view informational requirements of different types of clienteles. But, this service is yet to take off in the field of archives. For providing abstracting services, libraries usually prepare indicative and informative type of abstracts depending on requirements of its users. On the other hand, there are no such services available in the field of archives. However, the archives do prepare calendars and descriptive lists which serves some purpose of the researchers.

## 5.4 *Reference and Referral Services*

It is the solemn duty of the professions *i.e.* of archivists and librarians to help researchers by providing reference and referral services to facilitate their research by making available archival and library materials in course of conduct of their researches. It is needless to emphasise that published sources and the archival sources of information often supplement each other. The library and information centres have well established principles and techniques for the dissemination of information from their holdings. Archival information is also being disseminated in a number of ways. Most archival repositories, however, put reliance only on finding aids designed to assist both staff and researchers in the task of locating needful information. As far as libraries are concerned, most of them have necessary set up as well as required reference materials to render effective reference and referral services. Therefore, there is also a need for archival institutions to consider providing reference and referral services on the lines of libraries and information centres. For the purpose, there are some basic requirements for providing archival reference services:

*a*) Trained staff, knowledge about records and information contained therein in the repository and their potential users/ researchers.

*b*) Finding aids that will give essential information about the provenance, organisation and contents of the records;

*c*) Copying facilities for the quick use of the records.

## 5.5 *Long Range Reference Service*

Librarians have been a privileged lot because they are possessing a system for the standardisation and exchange of bibliographical data known as MARC which is being internationally used for providing reference services. But, archivists are facing problems in adoption of that very system MARC. They have, therefore, written a similar system known as MARC, AMC. However, in most developing countries the scenario is quite different and, as such, the very development of archival networks will certainly depend on the prior development of library and information network, which are still in its infancy, However, because of advent of new technology, it is quite possible that the development of general purpose computer network will in the long run necessitate development of either specialist exchange systems are adoption of archival data similar to that of library formats. The present reference service being provided in archival institutions is much different than what is being provided in Library and Information Centres. The archives are a short of unique record, as such, acquitance with them can only be acquired by working within archival institutions. The most of the users of library are already familiar with the publications house, therein and, therefore, depend on reference service with regard to type of publications and their contents. But, the users of an archive are disadvantaged lot, in the sense that they have to depend on reference service for everything as far as information contained in records are concerned. This implies that establishment of contact between right user and the right record requires one's familiarity with the records and also lenien sympathetic attitude towards exact needs of clienteles of archives.

### *5.6 Loan Service*

There is utmost need for closer cooperation in between Central and State archives in respect of inter-archives loan services on the very pattern of present inter-library loan services. On the very pattern of libraries, inter-archives loan services can be introduced particularly in finding aids to make a beginning.

### *5.7 Issue and Return of Publications and Records*

Issue and return of materials belonging to archives and libraries are common important activity. But, library techniques of issue and return of publications cannot be applied to record centres for issue of documents in their possessions, simply because library systems are based upon the premise that both document and clienteles can easily be identified.

However, in the archival context, the tasks are not identical in comparison to library in which items need to be identified in a box on the shelves; and access point and other restrictions are required to be checked. However, archival user services are required to be brought at par with that of library services, which can be possible only by introducing automation in their activity of issue and return of records. This will also enable archives to prepare a list of records which are over due for return.

### *5.8 Document Reproduction Service*

Basically, archives are reproduced in order to provide researchers with copies of the documents. But, now because of boost in the research activity, where more and more information is required by researchers from archives, being primary source of information, the need for providing quick copies of the material cannot be undermined. This has thrown a new challenge to the document reproduction service being provided by archival institutions. For the purpose, a full-fledged reprographic unit has become indispensable. The trend in archival institutions of developed countries show that the supply of copies in terms of pages are much more in comparison to supply of copies by their libraries. Therefore, none of the archival institutions of developing countries can any longer afford to under-estimate the value of providing quick document reproduction service. In addition to supply of copies to researchers, the document reproduction service can also be resorted to as a means of reducing the physical volumes of the records of archives. It is, therefore, much more necessary to provide fully equipped reprographic unit for both archives and libraries as this unit is vital for the effective functioning of both archives and libraries.

## *5.9 Copyright*

The copyright act should not be interpreted in the disadvantage of the bona fide researchers, simply as a lame excuse to discourage them while supplying copies of the publications housed in the libraries. As regards information contained in governmental record, these can be supplied to the bona fide researchers after ensuring that the information contained therein is not prejudicial to the interest of the state. However, the copy right act may strictly be enforced in case of certain publications, which contain control-vertical maps of the countries and other related information regarding territorial disputes.

## *5.10 Translation and Transcription Services*

To come to the rescue of researchers in overcoming the language barrier, the archivists should explore the possibility of rendering translation and transcription services on the pattern of libraries. For this purpose, various archives, national as well as state can get prepared a panel of translators of different languages in which plenty of records are available in their repository and there is demand for translation service. This service should be extended on no profit no loss basis to enable the researchers to make best use of materials in the languages not known to them. It must be ensured that the charges of translation and transcription are not prohibitive to potential users of information available in records.

## 6. Public Relations

The very objective of the archives like libraries should also be to serve those who come to utilise the documents in their possession. In this connection, it is mentioned that there are usually three kind of users, who come under the threshold of archives. Foremost among them are government organisations whose requirements need to be catered first by providing all available documents required in connection with official work. Thereafter, the archivist must give facilities to the general public to get requisite information and also to obtain copies of the records, etc. Finally, the archives need to discharge social obligations by looking after the interest of the research organisations and individual researchers.

### *6.1 Exhibition and Display of Records/Publications*

Till recently, the exhibitions were exclusively in the domain of librarians, as information contained in the governmental records was out of bound for common man. Therefore, the archivists seldom ventured out to exhibit government documents for information of common man. But because of the incoming democracies in most part of the world, the access to information in governmental records has also been recognised as a matter of right of individuals. To achieve this objective, the archivists are also taking keen interest in organising exhibitions on the pattern of librarians to apprise the public at large with special events, etc. The archivists like librarians are professional educators in a limited way although their educational background may include studies in archival sciences. They, in some cases lack the practical teaching experience necessary to assess the needs of "Teaching with Archives and to prepare archival material, which can motivate young researchers and to make them capable of understanding. Therefore, even a well organised archives exhibitions may not give desired result from educator's point of view. The frequent used method to present archival documents to public view at large is still continuing in displays. Truely speaking, the educational impact of the specialised exhibitions need to be well received. Most exhibitions are usually mounted on representative events which may exhibit documents taken from different archival repositories and also important pictures including museum objects. The archives usually mount exhibitions on certain occasions for commemoration of anniversaries, etc., to create public awareness. The aims of the archivist in this context essentially remains the communication of information available in documents.

## 7. Manpower Planning

Document handling and its care should be part and parcel of training programmes of each and every archives. For this purpose, repository staff need professional training in handling of materials. Therefore, they should be taught all the core skills and latest methods. Similarly, staff involved in photocopying or microfilming of archival materials need special training as they have to handle unusual type of materials which are quiet different in nature than that of the material of the library. Towards this end, there seems to be some gap in the training of archivists in comparison to the librarians. Therefore, archives administrators need to give due consideration into this phenomenon and to come to the rescue of younger archivists by detailing them for necessary advance training on the pattern of library and information personnel, which will enable them to cope with the challenges thrown by modern information industry. The librarians seem to be having considerable advantage over archivists as far as their training and qualifications are concerned. In numerical strength also the graduates in the field of librarianship are for above and can be counted in thousand, in comparison to professional graduates in the discipline of archives just being in hundreds. In the changing information scenario, there is utmost need to combine training institutions for archivists, librarians, documentalists as all these strive towards the same end. A library training mainly focuses attention on the treatment of individual item which is contrary to the principles of archives. These become much more acute when archives and manuscripts are kept under the charge of an archivist having just library training. Further, application of library rules for collection building may prove risky if it is applied to appraisal of public records. Similarly, library techniques of classification may give undesirable result if applied to classification of archival collections programme for providing training for archives and library personnel should be drawn on the basis of evaluation of manpower needs to ensure the standard performance of the tasks assigned.

## 8. Conclusion and Suggestion

To provide right information to the right reader, at the right time, in the right amount and in the right form should be the objective of information managers of archives, libraries and information centres. The traditional archival information services are also required to be replaced by modern techniques of documentation and dissemination of information. To achieve this end, archivists and librarians can benefit greatly from each other's experience. In this regard, librarians can study archivist's method of contents descriptions and archivists can study standard format, indexing language and thesaurus construction to which librarians and information scientists have given so much attention.

*Chapter 6*

# Right to Information: Role being Played by National Archives of India Library

## 1. Introduction

In today's information society, right to access to information is individual's birth right. In a number of countries, right to access to information and fundamental right go side by side ensuring individual's access to information and at the same time safeguarding privacy in case of private information. Hence, it is quite logical if persons demand that governmental information may be thrown open without any restriction for the purpose of research. Librarians' role as providers of information could change the scenario in variety of ways. They can act as information brokers, helping users to retrieve the information that they need to arrive at a decision and to complete a research.

## 2. Access to Information Available in the Holdings of National Archives of India Library

The objective of National Archives of India Library is to cater to the information requirements of decision makers, creators of records of Government of India, researchers of Modern Indian History, trainees of various courses run by the department, authors, writers, etc. The library provides secondary sources of information and functions as a useful adjunct to the government records available in the department. The library extends reference facility to the bona fide research scholars and thus facilitates researches particularly in Modern Indian History.

When in 1891, then Imperial Record Department (now known as National Archives of India) was established, a Central Library, as well as also visualised to function as an apex body of the Imperial Record Department and also to the various departmental libraries of Government of India. Consequently, a large number of books, periodicals and government publications were transferred to the Imperial Record Department to be kept in the proposed Central Library. But, in 1903, because of the creation of Imperial Library (now National Library) most of the publications from the Central Library were got transferred to it, leaving behind only duplicate copies of the publications. The then, Central Library became the Library of the Imperial Record Department and continued to function as a spare copy room. Transfer of holdings of the spare copy room from Calcutta to New Delhi was completed along with the public records in March, 1937, and this precious collection still forms part of about 2 lacs holdings of the National Archives of India Library.

The holdings of National Archives of India Library comprises of printed books; Gazettes; Gazetteers; Census Reports; Indian Administrative Reports; Parliamentary Debates; Legislative Assembly Debates; Provincial Legislative Council Debates; India Office List; Indian Army List; Civil List; Selections from Vernacular Native Newspapers; Selections from Records; East India Register and Directory; Times of India Directory; Almanacs; Collection of Treaties; Engagements and Sanads; Annual Register (Great Britain), Indian Annual Register. Besides these, Library possesses proscribed publications banned by the Raj, Fort William College Collection, Travelogues, Freedom Struggle Papers/ Books, etc. As such, it can boast to be one of the finest and richest repositories in the country.

As elsewhere in the country, the Library of the National Archives of India has also realised the need for quick dissemination of Information and is going in for Modern Information Technology in meeting the needs of its clientele. A beginning towards automation is going to be made shortly. The future goal of the Library is to gear itself to meet the ever growing information needs of decision makers and researchers.

## *2.1 Access to Governmental Information*

What librarians often call government information is available in the government documents. Each Ministry / Department brings out annual report, etc. for use and information of general public through their publication programme. Though the information contained therein is taken from the records, but as soon as the information is published, it becomes the part of the library material. The National Archives of India has published a number of documents for use and information of research scholars and others. Some of the notable publications are (*i*) Register of Private Records, (*ii*) Descriptive List of Secret Department Records, (*iii*) Descriptive List of Persian Correspondence, (*iv*) Guide to the Records in the National Archives of India, (*v*) Catalogue of Historical Maps of Survey of India (1700-1900), (*vi*) Catalogue of the Memoirs, (*vii*) Guide to the source of Asian History, (*viii*) Calendar of Acquired Documents, (*ix*) Annual Reports of National Archives, (*x*) Patriotic Poetry and Writing banned by the Raj, (*xi*) Resolutions of Indian Historical Records Commission, (*xii*) Selections from Educational Records, (*xiii*) Index to the press list of the Public Department Records, (*xiv*) Fort William India House correspondence.

## *2.2 Access through Information Systems and Services*

National Archives of India traditionally assists the users in two ways. The first is by providing an end-product in the shape of information required by the users. This is reference work whereby all necessary citations, monographs and similar materials are placed before the user. The second is by providing guidance to the readers/research scholars through various retrieval systems but essentially leaving to the user the responsibility for finding the required material/information.

## 2.3 *Classification of Information*

The library maintains a rich collection of classified documents issued by British Raj which are best source materials for the study of administration, history, military history, law, freedom struggle, etc. A list of notable government classified documents is given below:

| | |
|---|---|
| For Official Use Only | : Rules for the security of official documents and correspondence, 1938. |
| Confidential | : Routes in Persia, General Staff, India, 1928. |
| Confidential | : India and Communism Compiled in the Intelligence Bureau, Home Deptt, Govt. of India, 1933. |
| Security | : Military Report on Egypt, 1937. General Staff, The War Office, May, 1938. |
| Secret | : Report : The Present Military Position Gilgit by Captain, A. Durand, General Staff, Corps. Shimla, 1888. |

| | | |
|---|---|---|
| Secret | : | Communism in India by Celil Kaye, 1926. |
| Banned by | : | Gandhi Bigul (Poetry) |
| the Raj | : | Angrezon Se Meri Appeal (Writing) |

Most of the then classified documents available in the library are accessible for bona fide research. The exception being some of the banned publications which are inflammatory in nature arousing religious fantasy and also those which are pornographic literature.

## 3. Barriers on Access to Information

### *3.1 Orders Prohibiting Access to Certain Kind of Information*

Sometime even the publisher of the particular publication feel that the information contained in the publication may prove prejudicial to the interest of the country and endanger its security and sovereignty. As such, impose restriction by freezing the publication. The Survey of India had requested us in 1978 that its publication entitled *"Historical Records of the Survey of India, Volumes I to IV* by Col. R.H. Phillimore" should not be displayed publically. Similarly, the use of the publication entitled *"A Collection of Treaties, Engagements, and Sanads Relating to India and Neighbouring Countries," Volume 14*, compiled by C.U. Aitchison and published in 1929 is forbidden. The library is also not supplying copies of those pages from any publication in which old map of the country (India) is shown along with neighbouring countries depicting boundaries.

### *3.2 Restrictions Imposed by Creators of Certain Information*

There are certain publications, the copies of which are being received in the library. But, because of the direction from the creators of the publication, the information contained therein can not be shown to the users of the library. In this regard 'Army List 1990-1991' issued by the Ministry of Defence, Government of India can be cited as an example. The said publication has been marked RESTRICTED, with the direction that "the information given in this document is not to be communicated either directly or indirectly, to the press or to any person not authorised to receive it."

## 4. Use, Misuse and Abuse of Information by Some Users for their vested Interests

The users of National Archives of India Library have different level of informational requirement according to their disciplines, concepts of values and roles in society. Though the library provides requisite information to the persons to facilitate their research/task, but the possibility of information being misused and abused cannot be eliminated altogether. Therefore, before supplying copies of the information available in the published material, library takes an undertaking from the users not to sell, duplicate or transfer copies supplied to him/her by the National Archives of India to any other person without prior permission of the Director General of Archives; and suitably acknowledge the materials, if published and comply with the provisions of copyright, where applicable. Sometimes, persons are not fully conversant with copyright laws and think that because they have obtained copies of the materials from the National Archives of India, therefore, there is no need to seek prior permission from authors/publishers of the publications while inserting their materials in the publications. As a matter of fact, library is only custodian of the publications available in its holdings and provides extracts from the publications only for bona fide research, as copyright does not vest with it on those publications which have not been published by the National Archives of India. As a precautionary measure, the library does not entertain requests for the supply of the copies of a painting, a drawing, map, chart, an engraving or a photograph from the publications, as these possess artistic quality and come under copyright laws. These are mostly needed by the users for the purpose of insertion in their proposed publication and have no direct bearing on the research.

## 5. Special Role being Played by National Archives of India Library to Assist Decision Makers in their Decision-Making Process

Information involves reduction of uncertainty, that is what the decision maker expects from the information system. However, the degree of uncertainty of the decision maker will vary, and so the amount of information needed or taken from the system will vary. Since the latest trend in the government is towards the research-oriented decision–making, therefore, policy planners are also being catered like research scholars by the National Archives of India, of course, on priority basis. The National Archives of India serves government decision makers in the three wings i.e. legislature, executive and judiciary branches of Government of India through its library.

## 6. Conclusion

The National Archives of India Library has been contributing its mite to fulfil the objective of right to information by providing right information to the users at right time in the right amount and in the right form to facilitate bonafide research and decision–making. The access was debarred only in those cases where national security and integrity so demanded in holding the information from the individuals. To keep pace with the rapid development taking place in the field of information technology and to provide users oriented information services, the library has planned computerisation of its holdings and networking with libraries under Department of Culture with a view to make it a futuristic library gearing up to meet the evergrowing information needs of the researchers, decision-makers, etc., for 21st Century.

*Chapter 7*

# Role of National Archives of India Library in Providing Information to the Researchers, Decision Makers, etc.

The objective of National Archives of India Library is to provide timely and need-based services to decision makers. Creators of records of Government of India. Researchers of Modern Indian History, Trainees of various courses run by the department, authors, writers, etc. The library provides secondary sources of information and functions as a useful adjunct to the government records available in the department. The library extends reference facility to the bona fide Research Scholars and thus facilitates researches particularly in Modern Indian History.

When in 1891, then Imperial Record Department (now known as National Archives of India) was established, a central library, as well, was also visualised to function as an apex body of the Imperial Record Department and also to the various departmental libraries of the Government of India.

It was then thought that the keeper of the records, in addition to his duties of looking after the public records could also be entrusted with the responsibility of organising archival library and preparation of catalogues. Consequently, a large number of books. periodicals and government publications were transferred to the Imperial Record Department to be kept in the proposed Central Library. But, in 1903, because of the creation of Imperial Library (now National Library), most of the publications from the Central Library were got transferred to it, leaving behind only duplicate copies of the publications. The then, Central Library became the library of the Imperial Record Department and continued to function as a 'Spare Copy Room'. Transfer of holdings of the 'Spare Copy Room' from Calcutta to New Delhi was completed along with the public records in March, 1937, and this precious collection still forms parts of about 2 lacs holding of National Archives of India.

Like other libraries, the collection of National Archives of India Library is also being continuously enriched keeping in view the information requirements of its users. The making of an effective collection to attain the set goals of the department is a continuous process. However, in view of the limited resources available for acquisition of publications, the National Archives of India Library can achieve its objective through networking and resource sharing with government libraries located at New Delhi under Department of Culture. This will enable the Library as well as other participating libraries to meet the set goals of their departments effectively, and also to serve the users interest to its best, within a budget, which is seldom generous.

In the above context, it may be mentioned that in the past, there had been some attempt in this direction when the libraries of Central Secretariat Library Archaeological Survey of India Library, National Museum Library, National Archives Library had co-operated in the venture of preparation of an Union catalogue with the sole aim of resource sharing through inter-library loan. But the attempt could not make much headway perhaps due to non-availability of requisite staff; and as such the project was abandoned sometime in the beginning of 1980's. In that venture, libraries made a point to acquire most of the publications relating to the areas of their specific interest, and thus, enabling their respective departments to make optimum use of limited funds available for purchase of publications. The work of co-ordination of the committee of librarians was done by the Director of Central Secretariat Library, who was also its Chairman.

In pursuance of the recommendations of the Fourth Central Pay Commission, Government of India, Department of Culture vide their resolution dated 2nd September, 1987, appointed a Review Committee on Library Staff under the Chairmanship of Prof. D.P. Chattopadhyay. The Committee submitted its report in 1989, and on the basis of its recommendations,

Department of Expenditure, Ministry of Finance issued O.M. dated 24th July, 1990, introducing uniform rationalised pay structure for library staff. It also contained detailed guidelines identifying the parameters for categorisation of libraries on the basis of their collection, service, provided budget, publications and computer application. Accordingly, Government of India libraries have been grouped into six categories. Type I to V have been categorised on the basis of the variables; whereas category VI has been marked for the National Library, Calcutta. The review committee's basic thrust was to emphasise the changing role of a library from being just a storage point for library resources with provision for adequate access, tools and techniques for its retrieval to that of disseminator of information to all categories of users through various modern communication methods. The libraries were thus required to be linked up in a computer network as a modern, integrated library and information system.

Consequent upon the implementation of Ministry of Finance, Department of Expenditure O.M. No. F. 19(1) IC/86, dated 24.7.1990, Library of National Archives of India has been upgraded and placed under category III; and on the basis of this categorisation one post of librarian in the pre-revised pay scale of Rs. 2000-35000 was upgraded in the pay scale of Rs. 3000-4500 and designated as Library and Information Officer. The publications housed in National Archives of India Library form a significant part of nation's information resources. It is, therefore, essential that this library services also operate efficiently within the limitations of available resources. As the traditional manual information services can not cope up with the changing situation, therefore, these are required to be replaced by modern techniques of dissemination of information, modernisation implies application of computers for the dissemination of information.

It is noticed that the environment for library networks in India is picking up. However, the mute question before most of the Government of India Librarians is that of the cost which is most crucial factor to decide whether or not to replace manual system by automated systems. In most of the libraries where automation has been introduced are of the opinion that automation is advantageous both in financial terms and in the terms of change in the methods of work and attitudes of the staff. Keeping in view the worldwide revolution in the field of information and aspirations of its clientle, National Archives of India Library has gone for computerisation of its holdings which comprise of following notable publications in its precious collection of about 2 lacs publications:

1. Gazettes of India and Gazetteers.
2. Census of India Reports, 1871-till date.
3. Indian Administrative Reports, 1855-1933.
4. Parliamentary Debates.
5. Legislative Assembly Debates.

6. Provincial Legislative Council Debates.
7. Civil List, 1886-1989.
8. Selection of Vernacular Native Newspapers, 1863-1937.
9. Selection from Records of Government of India and State Governments.
10. East India Register and Directory, 1815-1860.
11. Times of India Directory, 1865-1983.
12. Almanacs.
13. Collection of Treaties, Engagements and Sanads compiled by C.U. Aitchison, 14 Volumes, 1900-1929.
14. Annual Register (Great Britain), 1877-1988.
15. Indian Annual Register, 1919-1947.
16. Proscribed Literature in English and Vernacular Languages.
17. Fort William College Collection.
18. Travelogues.
19. Journals/Periodicals/Bulletins relating to Archives and Modern Indian History.

The Library is co-operating with four libraries viz. Central Secretariat Library, Archaeological Survey of India Library, National Museum Library and National Gallery of Modern Art Library under Department of Culture in resource sharing programme, which has been established among these libraries to ensure optimum use of scarce resources. A proposal for networking among these libraries is underway which will facilitate the following:

— access to the participants' collection, services and databases through, say, Open Access Catalogue (OPAC) interfaces;
— knowing the content of the participants' catalogue databases particularly in the CD-ROM, whenever and wherever it is required;
— library and information service users' access to other databases available in, say, online hosts, CD-ROM or via OPAC;
— the exchange of indexes and bibliographic records particularly using CD-ROM facilities;
— the exchange and sharing of documents and other related library and information service activities among the cooperating members, including sharing the expenses and tasks involved in creating and sustaining databases; and
— the provision of specialist services such as electronic mail (E-Mail), file transfer, and directory services within the frame of document delivery services.

The WAN (Wide Area Network) system is also underway to connect these five libraries. It would be operational online in distributed system.

The automated library network will facilitate the following activity:

(*i*) charge and discharge library materials and signal over-borrowing without undue delay;
(*ii*) renew, reserve, recall and hold/trap library

materials for the use of other prospective library clientele/member libraries;

(*iii*) identify legitimate and delinquent clientele particularly during charging/discharging of the library materials;

(*iv*) periodically prepare and print accurate and detailed statistical analysis and lists of the registered clientele; member libraries; frequency of library use; frequency of library stock consulted; number of materials loaned to the clientele; number of materials despatched or received from other libraries within and outside the country on loan/exchange; number of materials placed on order-received/bills settled; number of materials placed on reserve; damaged, missing sent for repairs or binding; temporarily withdrawn or needed out of the library, etc.

(*v*) automatically update amend information about the library books/documents; clientele; book suppliers, subscription agents, etc. Such information should include: new accessions; change of call members; change of addresses; change of clientele's identification number; ceasure of the clientele's relationship with the parent institution of the member libraries, etc.

# References


Abraham, Terry, Balzarini, Stephne E. and Frantilla, Anne: What is backlog is prologue; a measurement of archival processing. American Archivist, vol. 48, no. 1.

Alexander, D.: A description of indexing procedures for the "Agreement on Account of Crew", Archives, vol. 11, 1973, pp. 86-93.

Alldredge, E.O.: Inventorying magnetic-media records, American Archivists, vol. 35, 1972, pp. 337-45.

Allen, C.G.: Central African archives: some aspects of their development. The Indian Archives, vol. 2, no. 1, January 1948.

Allen, Marie: Optical character recognition: technology with new relevance for archival automation, American Archivists, vol. 50, no. 1, Winter 1987, pp. 88-99.

Andrews, Patricia A., comp: Writings on archives, historical manuscripts, and current records: 1983. American Archivist, vol. 49, no. 3, Summer 1986, pp. 277-303.

Angel, Herbert E.: Archival janus: the records center. American Archivist, vol. 31, no. 1, January 1968, pp. 5-12.

Arad, A. and Bell, L.: Archival description-a general system, ADPA, vol. 2, 1978, pp. 2-9.

Basu, Purnendu: Records and archives: what are they? The Indian Archives, vol. 2, nos. 2-4, April. July and October 1948, pp. 75-81.

Basu, Purnendu: Why preserve records ? The Indian Archives, vol. 3, Nos. 1-4, January-December 1949, pp, 88-95.

Baumann, Roland M: The administration of access to confidential records in state archives: common practices and the need for a model law. American Archivist, vol. 49, no. 4, Fall 1986, pp. 349-69.

Bearman, David A. and Lytle, Richard H: The power of the principle of provenance. Archivaria, no. 21, Winter 1985-86, pp. 14-27.

Bearman, David: Towards national information systems for archives and manuscripts repositories: the national information system task force (NISTF) papers. Chicago, Society of American Archivists, 1987.

Bechor, Malvina B: Bibliographic access to archival literature. American Archivist, vol. 50, no. 2, Spring 1987, pp. 243-47.

Bell, Harold Idris: The custody of records in Roman Egypt. The Indian Archives, vol. 4, no. 2, July-December 1950, pp. 116-25.

Bell, L.: The archival implications of machine-readable records, Archivum, vol. 26, 1979, pp. 85-92.

Berner, Richard C. and Haller, Uli: Principles of archival inventory construction. American Archivist, vol. 47, no. 2, Spring 1984, pp. 134-55.

Berner, Richard C: Arrangement and description: some historical observations. American Archivist, vol. 41, no. 2, April 1978, pp. 169-81.

Binkley, Robert C: Strategic objectives in archival policy. American Archivist, vol. 2, no. 3, July 1939, pp. 162-68.

Boberach, H. and Buchmann, W.: Advanced technologies and the expansion of archives access. Archivum, vol. 26, 1979, pp. 127-36.

Boer, D.: 'Business archives in automated information retrieval systems', Archivum, vol. 18, 1968, pp. 191-98.

Boles, Frank and Young, Julia Marks: Exploring the black box: the appraisal of university administrative records. American Archivist, vol. 48, no. 2, Spring 1985, pp. 121-40.

Boles, Frank: Disrespecting original order. American Archivist, vol. 45, no. 1, Winter 1982, pp. 26-32.

Boles, Frank: Sampling in archives. American Archivist, vol. 44, no. 2, Spring 1981, pp. 125-30.

Born, Lester K.: Baldassare Bonifacio and his essay "De Archivis". American Archivist, vol. 4, no. 4, October 1941, pp. 221-37.

Brauer, Carl M: Researcher evaluation of reference service. American Archivist, vol. 43, no. 1, Winter 1980, pp. 77-79.

Brichford, Maynard: Archives and manuscripts: appraisal and accessioning. Chicago, Society of American Archivists, 1977.

British Standards Institution: BS 5408: Glossary of documentation terms, BSI, 1977.

Brooks, Philip C: Archivists and their colleagues: common denominators. American Archivist, vol. 14, no. 1, January 1951, pp. 33-44.

Brooks, Phillip C: The selection of records for preservation. American Archivist, vol. 3, no. 4, October 1940, pp. 221-34.

Buchanan, S.A.: Disaster planning, preparedness and recovery for libraries and archives: a RAMP study (PGI-88/ws/6). Paris: UNESCO, 1988.

Buck, Solon J: Let's look at the record. American Archivist. vol. 8, no. 2, April 1945, pp. 109-14.

Burke, Frank G: Archival co-operation. American Archivist, vol. 46., no. 3, Summer 1983, pp. 293-305.

Burke, R Frank G: The future course of archival theory in the United States. American Archivist, vol. 44, no. 1, Winter 1981, pp. 40-46.

Calmes, A.: 'Practical realities of computer based finding aids: the NARS A-1 experience'. American Archivists, vol. 42, 1979, pp. 167-77.

Cappon, Lester J: What, then, is there to theorize about ? American Archivist, vol. 45, no. 1, Winter 1982, pp. 19-25.

Casterline, Gail Farr: Archives and manuscripts: exhibits. Chicago, Society of American Archivists, 1980.

Chalmers, Duncan: Computer indexing in the Public Record Office. The Indian Archives, vol. 30, no. 1, January-June 1983, pp. 55-73.

Chapman, Patricia: Guidelines on preservation and conservation policies in the archives and libraries heritage: a RAMP study (PGI-90/ws/7). Paris: UNESCO, 1990.

Charlton, Thomas L.: Videotaped oral histories: problems and prospects. American Archivists, vol. 47, no. 3, Summer 1984, pp. 238-236.

Chowdhari, G.G.: Natural language processing and information retrieval: Basic issues, ASLIC Bulletin, vol. 6 (2): pp. 45-50.

Christian, John F. and Finnegan, Shonnie: On planning an archives. American Archivist, vol. 37, no. 4, October 1974, pp. 573-78.

Clarke, R.L.: 'Standardization and technology'. In Archive-Library relations, ed. R.L. Clarke, Bowker, New York/ London, 1976, pp. 133-40.

Clements, D.W.G.: preservation and conservation of library documents: A UNESCO/IFLA/ICA enquiry into the current staff of the world's patrimony: a RAMP study (PGI-87/ws/15). Paris: UNESCO, 1987.

Clements, D.W.G.: Review of training needs in preservation and conservation: (PGI-89/ws/15). Paris , UNESCO, 1989.

Connor, R.D.W.: Adventurers of an amateur archivist. American Archivist, vol 6, no. 1, January 1943, pp. 1-18.

Conway, Paul: Facts and frameworks: an approach to studying the users of archives. American Archivist, vol. 49, no. 3, Fall 1986, pp. 393-407.

Conway, Paul: Perspectives on archival resources: the 1985 census of archival institutions. American Archivists, vol. 50. no. 2, Spring 1987, pp. 174-91.

Cook, Michael: Information management and archives data. London: Library Association, 1993.

Cook, Michael: Introduction to archival automation: a RAMP study (PGI-86/ws/15). Paris: UNESCO, 1986.

Cook, Michael: Management of information from archives. Aldershot, Grower, 1986.

Cook, Michael and Procter: Management, Manual of archival description. Aldershot, Grower, 1989.

Cook, Michael: Archives and the computer, 2nd ed. London, Buttrworths, 1986.

Cook, Michael: Professional training: international perspectives. Archivaria, no. 7, Winter 1978, pp. 28-40.

Cook, Micheal: Archives administration: a manual for intermediate and smaller organizations and for local government. Aldershot, WM Dawson, 1977.

Cook, Micheal: An introduction to archival automation: a RAMP study with guidelines. Paris, UNESCO, 1986.

Cook, Terry: Archival appraisal of records containing personal information: a RAMP study with guidelines (PGI-91/ws/3). Paris: UNESCO, 1991.

Cooper, M.D.: Usage patterns of an online search system, Journal of the American Society for Information Science, 31 (5) 1983, pp. 343-49.

Cooper, W.S.: A definition of relevance for information retrieval. Information storage and retrieval, vol. 7, 1971, pp. 19-37.

Cox, Richard J.: Professionalism and archivists in the United States. American Archivist, vol. 49, no. 3, Summer 1986, pp. 229-47.

Cox, Richard J: American archival history: its development, needs, and opportunities. American Archivist, vol. 46, no. 1, Winter 1983, pp. 31-41.

Cox, Richard J: Bibliography and reference for the archivist, American Archivist, vol. 46, no. 2, Spring 1983, pp. 185-87.

Crawford, Michael J. Copyright: Unpublished manuscripts, and the archivist. American Archivist, vol. 46, no. 2, Spring 1983, pp. 135-47.

Crespo, Carmen and Vinas, Vicente: The preservation and restoration of paper records and books: a RAMP study with guidelines. Paris, UNESCO, 1984.

Crooks, Joyce: Civil Liberties, Libraries and Computers, Libr, J. (Feb. 1, 1976). pp. 482.

Cunha, George M: Methods of evaluation to deter-mine the preservation needs in libraries and archives: a RAMP study (PGI-88/ws/16). Paris: UNESCO, 1988.

Davis, W.N., Jr.: Budgeting for archival processing. American Archivist, vol. 42, no. 2, Spring 1980, pp. 209-11.

Dearstyne, Bruce W: Principles for local government records: a statement of the National Association of

State Archives and Records Administrators. American Archivist, vol. 46, no. 4, Fall 1983, pp. 452-57.

Dearstyne, Bruce W: What is the 'use' of archives ? a challenge for the profession. American Archivist, vol. 50, no. 1., Winter 1987, pp. 76-87.

DePuy, LeRoy: Archivists and records managers-a partnership. American Archivist, vol. 23, no. 1, January 1960, pp. 49-55.

Devarajan, G. (Ed.), (1990): Library computerisation in India, New Delhi, ESS Publications.

Dewhiti, B.: 'Archival uses of computers in the US and Canada'. American Archivists, vol. 42, 1979, p. 152, 57.

Dodds, Gordon: Back to square one-records management revisited. Archivaria, vol. 1, no. 2, Summer 1976, pp. 88-91.

Dollar, Charles M.: Appraising machine-readable records. American Archivists, vol. 41, no. 4, October 1978. 423-30.

Dollar, Charles M.: Electronic records management and archives in international organizations: a RAMP study with guidelines. Paris, UNESCO, 1986.

Doyle, Murielle: Preparation of records management handbooks for government agencies: a RAMP study (PGI-91/ws/18). Paris: UNESCO, 1991.

Duboscq, Guy: The educational role of the archives. UNESCO Bulletin for Libraries, vol. 24, July-August 1970, pp. 205-10.

Duchein, Michael: Archives at the service of the administration of the researcher, and of the private citizen, The Indian Archives, vol. 27, no. 2, July-December 1978, pp. 1-13.

Duchein, Michel: obstacls to the access, use and transfer of information from archives: a RAMP study, Paris. UNESCO, 1983.

Duchein, Michel: Theoretical principles and practical problems of repsect des fonds in archival science. Archivaria, no. 16, summer 1983, pp. 64-82.

Duniway, David C: Conflicts in collecting. American Archivist, vol. 24, no. 1, January 1961, pp. 55-63.

Durr, W. Theodore: some thoughts and designs about archives and automation, 1984. American Archivist, vol. 47, no. 3, Summer 1986, pp. 6-98.

Ehrenberg, Ralph E.: Archives and manuscripts: maps and architectural drawings. Chicago, Society of American Archivists, 1982.

Ellis, Roger H: The British archivist and his training. Journal of the Society of Archivists, vol. 3, no. 6, Octo. 1967, pp. 265-71.

Enwere, J.C.: Arrangement of public records in Nigeria. The Indian Archives, vol. 32, no. 1, January-June 1983, pp. 11-26.

Evans, Frank B, com: Promoting archives and research: a study in international co-operation. American archivists vol. 50, no. 1, Winter 1987, pp. 48-65.

Evans, Frank B., comp: Modern archives and manuscripts: a select bibliography. Chicago, Society of American Archivists, 1975.

Evans, Frank B., comp: Modern archives and manuscripts: a select bibliography. Chicago, Society of American Archivists, 1975.

Evans, Frank B.: Archivists and records managers: variations on a theme. American Archivist, vol. 30, no. 1, January 1967, pp. 45-58.

Evans, Frank B.: Guidelines for surveying archival and records management systems and services: a RAMP study (PGI-83/ws/6). Paris: UNESCO, 1983.

Evans, Frank B.: Writings on archives published by and with the assistance of UNESCO: A RAMP study. Paris, UNESCO, 1983.

Evans, Frank B: Indian archival trainning and the archival training needs of Asia: some observations. The Indian Archives, vol. 30, no. 2, July-Dec. 1981, pp. 1-14.

Evans, Frank B: Postappointment archival training: a proposed solution for a basic problem. American Archivist, vol. 40, no. 1, January 1977, pp. 57-74.

Evans, Max: Authority control: an alternative to the record group concept. American Archivist, vol. 49, no. 3, Summer 1986, p. 249-61.

Field, B.J.: A thesaurus-based indexing and classification system developed for INSPEC product and services, Journal of Documentation, vol. 30, 1974, pp. 1-17.

Filipelli, R.L.: Oral history and the archives. American Archivist, vol. 39, no. 4, October 1976, pp. 479-83.

Finnegan, Ruth: A note on oral tradition and historical evidence. History and Theory, vol. 9. no. 2, 1970, pp. 195-201.

Fishbein, M.H.: 'ADP and archives: selected publications on automatic data processing'. American Archivist, vol. 38, 1975, pp. 31-42.

Fishbein, M.H.: 'Automation in archives: a summary history'. ADPA, vol. 3, 1981, pp. 9-13.

Fishbein, M.H.: Appraising information in machine-language form, American Archivists, vol. 35, 1972, pp. 35-43.

Fishbein, M.H.: Model curriculum for the education and training of Archivists in automation: a RAMP study (PGI-85 / ws / 27). Paris: UNESCO, 1985.

Fishbein, M.H.: The evidential value of non-textual records, American Archivists, vol. 45, 1982, pp. 189-90.

Fishbein, Meyer H: A viewpoint on the appraisal of national records. American Archivist, vol. 33, no. 2, April 1970, pp. 175-87.

Fishbeinq, Meyer H.: A model curriculum for the education and training of archivists in automation: a RAMP study, Paris, UNESCO, 1985.

Fishbeinq, Meyer H.: Guidelines for administering machine-readable archives. Washington, D.C., Committee on Automation, International Council on Archives, 1980.

Fisher, B. and Evans, F.B.: 'Automation, information and administration of archives and manuscript collection: a bibliographic review', American Archivists, vol. 30, 1967, pp. 333-48.

Fleckner, John A: Cooperation as a strategy for archival institutions. American Archivists, vol. 39, no. 4, October 1976, pp. 447-59.

Ford, Helen: Education of staff and users for the proper handling of archival materials: a RAMP study (PGI-91/ws/17). Paris: UNESCO, 1991.

Fox, M.J.: The Wisconsin machine-readable records project, American Archivists, vol. 47, 1981, pp. 429-31.

Franz, Eckhart G: Archives and education: a RAMP study with guidelines. Paris, UNESCO. 1986.

Freeman (Freivogel), Elsie T: Education programmes: Outreach as an administrative function. American, vol. 41, no. 2, April 1978, pp. 147-53.

Freeman, Elsie T: In the eye of the beholder: archives administration from the user's point of view. American Archivist, vol. 47, no. 2, Spring 1984, pp. 111-23.

Garay, K.E.: Access and copyright in literary collections. Archivaria, no. 18, Summer 1984, pp. 220-27.

Geselbracht, Raymond H: The origin of restrictions on access to personal papers at the Library of Congress and the National Archives. American Archivist, vol. 49, no. 2, Spring 1986, pp. 142-62.

Ghose, Sailen: Archives in India. Calcutta: Firma K.K. Mukhopadhyay, 1963.

Ghosh, Pradyot Kumar: Archives for everybody. The Indian Archives, vol. 28, Nos. 1-2, January-December 1979, pp. 32-36.

Giusti, Martino, The Vatican secret archives. Archivaria, no.7, Winter 1978. pp. 16-27.

Gracy, David B., II: Archives and manuscripts: arrangement and description. Chicago, Society of American Archivists, 1977.

Griffiths, Jose-Marie: Application of minicomputers and microcomputers to information handling: (PGI-81/ws/28). Paris: UNESCO, 1981.

Grimstead, Patricia Kennedy: Lenin's archival decree of 1918: the Bolshevik legacy for Soveit archival theory and practice. American Archivist vol. 45, no. 4, Fall 1982, pp. 429-43.

Grimstead, Patricia Kennedy: Regional archives development in the USSR: Soviet standards and national documentary legacies. American Archivist, vol. 36, no. 1, January 1973, pp. 43-66.

Grover, Ray: The National Archives of New Zealand: its historical context. Archivaria, no. 18, Summer 1984, pp. 232-40.

Grover, Wayne C: Archives: society and profession. American Archivist, vol. 18, no. 1, January 1955, pp. 3-10.

Grover, Wayne C: Archives: Society and profession. American Archivist, vol. 18, no. 1, January 1955, pp. 3-10.

Grover, Wayne C: The archivist's code. American Archivist, vol. 18, no. 4, October 1955, pp. 307-08.

Gupta, Pawan K. and Usha Pawan: Library and information sciences: current trends in india. Jaipur: RBSA, 1986.

Gupta, R.C.: Training of archivists in south and west Asia. The India Archives, vol. 31, no. 1, January-June 1982, pp. 1-24.

Guptil, Marilla B: Archival appraisal of records of international organisations: a RAMP study (PGI-85 /ws/9). Paris: UNESCO, 1985.

Gwiazda, Henry J., II: Preservation, decision-making and archival photocopying: twentieth century collections at the Kennedy Library. Restaurator, vol. 8, May 1987, pp. 55-62.

Hackman, Larry J. and Warnow-Blewett, Joan: The documentation strategy process: a model and a case study. American Archivist, vol. 50, no. 1, Winter 1987, pp. 12-47.

Haller, Uli: Variations in the processing rates on the Magnuson and Jackson senatorial papers. American Archivist, vol. 50, no. 1, Winter 1987, pp. 100-109.

Ham, F. Gerald: Archival strategies for the post-custodial era. American Archivist, vol. 44, no. 3, Summer 1981, pp. 207-16.

Hammitt, J.J.: Government archives and records management. American Archivist, vol. 28, no. 2, April 1965, pp. 219-22.

Harrod, Leonard Montague: Harrod's librarians, glossary of terms used in librarianship, documen-tation and the book crafts and reference book, Aldershot: Gower, 1987.

Harter, Stephen P.: Online information retrieval concepts, principles and techniques. San Diego, California: Academic Press, 1986.

Hedstrom, Margaret L: Archives and manuscripts:

machine-readable records. Chicago, Society of American Archivists, 1984.

Heine, M.H.: Distance between sets as an objective measure of retrieval effectiveness. Information storage and retreival, vol. 9, 1973, pp. 181-98.

Helfenstein, Ulrich: Swiss archives. American Archivist, vol. 37, no. 4, October, 1974, pp. 565-71.

Helmuth, Ruth W: Education for American Archivists: a view from the trenches. American Archivist, vol. 44, no. 3, Fall 1981, pp. 295-303.

Hendriks, Klaus B.: Preservation and restoration of photographic materials in archives and libraries: a RAMP study (PGI-84/ws/1). Paris: UNESCO, 1984.

Hensen, Steven L.: The use of standards in the application of the AMC format. American Archivist, vol. 49, no. 1, Spring 1987, pp. 31-40.

Hesselager, Lise: Fringe or grey literature in the national library: on 'papyrolatry' and the growing similarity between the materials in libraries and archives. American Archivists, vol. 47, no. 3, Summer 1984, pp. 255-70.

Hickerson, H. Thomas: Archives and manuscripts: an introduction to automated access. Chicago, Society of American Archivists, 1984.

Hodson, J.H.: Administration of archives. Oxford, Pergamon, 1972.

Hoff-Wilson, Joan: Access to restricted collections: the responsibility of professional historical organizations. American Archivists, vol. 46, no. 4, Fall 1983, pp. 441-47.

Holbert, Sue E: Archives and manuscripts: reference and access. Chicago, Society of American Archivists, 1977.

Holmes, Oliver W.: Archival arrangement-five different operations at five different levels. American Archivist, vol. 27, no. 1, January 1964, pp. 21-41.

Holmes, Oliver W: Public records: who knows what they are ? American Archivists, vol. 23, no. 1, January 1960, p. 3-26.

Horder, Alan: Guidelines for the care and preservation of microforms in tropical countries: (PGI-90/ws/17). Paris, UNESCO, 1990.

Ibid, vol. I, No. 4, 1947, pp. 289-93.

International Council on Archives: 'Mechanization, automation, data processing'. Basic international bibliography of archive administration, ed. by M. Duchein, Archivum, vol. 25, 1978, pp. 122-27.

Jackson, B.: A records management program. Records Management, vol. 5, 1981, pp. 8-32.

Jenkinson, Hilary: Selected writings of Sir Hilary Jenkinson. Gloucester, Alan Sutton, 1980.

Jenkinson, Hilary: 25 years: some reminiscences of an English archivist 1923-48. The Indian Archives, vol. 3, nos. 1-4. January-December 1949, pp. 12-35.

Joyce, William L: Archivists and research use. American Archivist, vol. 47, no. 2, Spring 1984, pp. 124-133.

Kaher, William J: The use of user studies. The Midwestern Archivist, vol. 11, no. 1, 1986, pp. 15-26.

Kahn, Herman: Some comments on the archival vocation. American Archivist, vol. 34, no. 1, January 1971, pp. 3-12.

Kahn, Herman: The long-range implications for historians and archivists of the charges against the Franklin D. Roosevelt Library. American Archivist, vol. 34, no. 3, July 1971, pp. 265-75.

Kathpalia, Y.P.: Model curriculum for training of specialists in document preservation and restoration: A RAMP study with guidelines (PGI-84/ws/ 2). Paris: UNESCO, 1984.

Kennedy, Bruce M: Confidentiality of Library Records: A survey of problems, policies, and laws, vol. 81, L. Libr, J. 1989 p. 733.

Keon, Jim: The Canadian archivist and copyright legislation. Archivaria, no. 18, Summer 1984, pp. 91-98.

Kepley, Brenda Beasley: Archives accessibility for the disabled. American Archivist, vol. 46, no. 1, Winter 1983, pp. 42-51.

Kepley, David R: Sampling in archives: a review. American Archivist, vol. 47, no. 3, Summer 1984, pp. 237-42.

Kesner, R.M.: Automation, Machine-readable records and archival administration: an annotated bibliography. Society of American Archivists, Chicago 1980.

Kesner, Richard M: Information management: machine-readable records and administration: an annotated bibliography. Chicago. Society of American Archivists, 1983.

Ketelaar, Eric: Archival and records management legislation and regulations: a RAMP study with guidelines. Paris, UNESCO, 1985.

Kitching, Christopher: Impact of computerization of archival finding aids: a RAMP study (PGI-91/ws/ 16). Paris, UNESCO, 1991.

Kromnow, Ake: The appraisal of contemporary records. Archivum. vol. 26, 1979, pp. 45-54.

Lacy, M. (1993): Understanding Computer Systems Architecture, New Delhi, BPB Publications.

Ladeira, Caroline Durant and Trautman, Maryellen, comps: Writings on archives, historical manuscripts, and current records: 1984. American Archivist, vol. 49, no. 4, Fall 1986, 425-54.

Lamb, G.H.: Computers in the Public Service, Allen and Unwin, London, 1973.

Lamb, W. Kaye: The changing role of the archivist. American Archivist, vol. 29, no. 1, January 1966, pp. 3-10.

Lancaster, F. Wilfred and Lindac Smith: Compati-bility issues affecting information systems and services: a RAMP study (PGI-83/ws/23). Paris: UNESCO, 1983.

Lathrop, Alan K: Copyright of architectural records: a legal perspective. American Archivist, vol. 49, no. 4, Fall 1986, pp. 409-23.

Lathrop, Alan K: The provenance and preservation of architectural records. American Archivists, vol. 43, no. 3, Summer 1980, pp. 325-26.

Leary, William H.: Archival appraisal of photographs: a RAMP study (PGI-85/ws/10), Paris, UNESCO, 1985.

Leavitt, Arthur H: What are archives ? American Archivist, vol. 24, no. 2, April 1961, pp. 175-78.

Lee, Charles E. Persons, places, and papers: The joys of being an archivist. American Archivist, vol. 36, no. 1, January 1973, p. 5-14.

Lee, Mary Wood: Preservation and treatment of mold of library collections with an emphasis on tropical climates: a RAMP study (PGI-88/ws/9). Paris: UNESCO, 1988.

Lewinson, Paul: Archival sampling. American Archivist, vol. 20, no. 4, October 1957, pp. 291-12.

Lodolini, Elio: Archivies organization in Italy. The Indian Archives, vol. 32, no. 1, January-June 1983, pp. 27-30.

Lokke, Carl: Archives and the French Revolution, American Archivists, vol. 31, no. 1, January 1968, pp. 23-31.

Lucas, Lydia: Efficient finding aids: developing a system for control of archives and manuscripts. American

Archivist, vol. 44, no. 1, Winter 1981, pp. 21-26.

Lytle, Richard H: Intellectual access to archives: second. report of an experiment comparing provenance and content indexing methods of subject retrieval. American Archivist, vol. 43, no. 2, Spring 1980, pp. 191-207.

Lytle, Richard, ed: Management of archives and manuscript collections for librarians. Chicago, Society of American Archivists, 1980.

Madan, P.L.: Record character of maps and related problems. The Indian Archives, vol. 31, no. 2, July-December 1982, pp. 13-22.

Madan, Som Nath (1987): Computer and Library Services, Delhi, Commonwealth Publishers.

Maher, W.J.: 'Administering archival automation: development of inhouse systems'. American Archivists, vol. 47, 1984, pp. 405-17.

Majumdar, J.S.: Neo-dynamics of records management: disposition of government records. The Indian Archives, vol. 31, no. 1, January-June 1983, pp. 46-54.

Mason, Philip P: Archives in the seventies: promises and fulfillment. American Archivist, vol. 44, no. 3, Summer 1981, pp. 199-206.

Mazikana, Peter C: Archives and records manage-ment for decision makers: a RAMP study (PGI-90/ws/8). Paris: UNESCO, 1990.

McCain, William D.: The value of records. American Archivist, vol. 16, no. 1, January 1953, pp. 3-11.

McCrank, Lawrence J: Prospects for integrating historical & information studies in archival education. American Archivist, vol. 42, no. 4, Oct., 1979, pp. 443-55.

Modern archives administration and records management: a RAMP study (PGI-85/ws/32). Paris: UNESCO, 1985.

Moltke-Hansen, David: Reflections on the problems of access to archival literature. American Archivist, vol. 47, no. 3, Summer 1984, pp. 293-95.

Morton, Katherine D.: The MARC formats: an overview. American Archivist, vol. 49, no. 1, Winter 1986, pp. 21-30.

Moser, A: 'Information concepts', Journal of documentation, vol. 34, 1978, pp. 350-5.

Moss, William W.: Archives in the People's Republic of China. American Archivist, vol. 45, no. 4, Fall 1982, pp. 385-409.

Mukhopadhyaya, A.: Experimental design of a bibliographical database with variable structure field length for dBase III plus applications, IASLIC Bulletin, vol. 34 (2): pp. 69-76.

Nair, R. Raman, (1992): Computer application to library and information services, New Delhi, ESS Publications.

Naugler, H.: Focus: the machine-readable archives division of the Public Archives of Canada, record projects, Archivaria, vol. 46, 1978, pp. 176-80.

Naugler, Harold: The appraisal of machine-readable records: a RAMP study with guidelines, Paris, UNESCO, 1984.

Nauman, Ann K., The Archivo General De Indias. Archives, vol. 15, no. 68, October 1982, p. 216-23.

New Encyclopaedia Britanica. Chicago: Encyclopaedia Britanica, Inc., 1985. Vol. 22 (Macro-paedia).

Oddy, R.N.: 'Information retrieval through man-machine dialogue', Journal of documentation, vol. 33, 1977, pp. 1-14.

Ormsby, William G.: The Public Archives of Canada, 1948-68. Archivaria, no. 15, Winter 1982-83, pp. 36-46.

Orr, William J: Archival training in Europe. American Archivist, vol. 44, no. 1, Winter 1981, pp. 27-39.

Palmer , M: Archive packs for schools: some practical suggestions. Journal of the Society of Archivists, vol. 6, no. 3, April 1979, pp. 145-53.

Parker, Thomas A: Study on integrated management for libraries and archives: a RAMP study (PGI-88 / ws / 20). Paris: Unesco, 1988.

Peace, Nancy E. and Chundacoff, Nancy Fisher: Archivists and librarians: a common mission, a common education. American Archivist, vol. 42, no. 4, October 1979, pp. 456-62.

Pederson, Ann E. and Casterline, Gail Farr: Archives and manuscripts: public programs. Chicago, Society of American Archivists, 1982.

Pederson, Ann E: Archival outreach: SAA's 1976 survey, American Archivists, vol. 41, no. 2, April 1978, pp. 155-62.

Peterson, Gary M. and Peterson, Trudy Huskamp: Archives and manuscripts: law. Chicago, Society of American Archivists, 1985.

Peterson, Gary M. and Peterson, Trudy Huskamp: Archives and manuscripts: law. Chicago, Society of American Archivists, 1985.

Peterson, T.H.: Archival principles and records of the new technology, American Archivists, vol. 47, 1984, pp. 383-93.

Peterson, Trudy Huskamp: Archival principles and records of the new technology. American Archivist, vol. 47, no. 4, Fall 1984, pp. 383-93.

Peterson, Trudy Huskamp: the deed and the fight. American Archivist, vol. 42, no. 1, January, 1979, pp. 61-79.

Peterson, Trudy Huskamp: The National Archives and the archival theorist revisited, 1954-84. American Archivist, vol. 49, no. 2, Spring 1986, pp. 125-33.

Phillips, Faye: Developing collecting policies for manuscript collections. American Archivist, vol. 47, no. 1, Winter 1984, pp. 30-42.

Pinkett, Harold T: American archival theory: the state of the art. American Archivist, vol. 44, no. 3, Summer 1981, pp. 217-22.

Polenberg, Richard: The Roosevelt Library case: a review article, American Archivist, vol. 34, no. 3, July 1955, pp. 277-84.

Posner, Ernst: The National Archives and the archival theorist. American Archivist, vol. 18, no. 3., July 1955, pp. 207-16.

Postner, Ernst.: Archives in medieval Islam. American Archivist, vol. 35, Nos. 3-4, July-October 1972, pp. 291-316.

Postner, Ernst: Some aspects of archival development since the French Revolution. American Archivist, vol. 3, no. 3, July, 1940. pp, 159-72.

Powers, Sandra: Why exhibit ? the risks versus the benefits. American Archivists, vol. 41, no. 3, July 1978, pp. 297-306.

Prasad, S.N.: Archives in India. Archivaria, no. 7, Winter 1978, pp. 52-60.

Pratt, A.D.: 'Information concepts', Journal of documentation, vol. 34, 1978, pp. 242-24.

Pugh, Mary Jo: The illusion of omniscience: subject access and the reference archivist. American Archivist, vol. 45, no. 1, Winter 1982, pp. 33-44.

Purdy, Virginia C: Archivaphobia: its causes and cure. Prologue, vol. 15, no. 2, Summer 1983, pp. 114-19.

Radoff, Morrif L: What should bind us together ? American Archivist, vol. 19, no. 1, January 1956, pp. 3-9.

Ranganathan, S.R.: Laws of archival science, Indian Archives, vol. I, No. 3, 1947, pp. 206-12.

Rao, D.N.: Automation of serial department in speical libraries, Lucknow Librarian, vol. 22 (1-2), pp. 17-27.

Rao, I.K. Ravichandra (1990): Library Automation, New Delhi, Wiley Eastern Ltd.

Rapport, Leonard: No grandfather clause: Reappraising accessioned records. American Archivist, vol. 44, no. 2, Spring 1985, pp. 143-50.

Rapport, Paul: Archival sampling. American Archivist, vol. 20, no. 4, October 1957, pp. 291-12.

Reed, D.: The RLIN AMC format: an experiment in library compatible archival data automation, Journal of the Society of Archivists.

Reingold, Nathan: Confessions of a reformed archivist. American Archivist, vol. 31, no. 4, October 1968, pp. 371-377.

Reitman, Alan: Freedom of information and privacy: the civil libertarin's dilemma. American Archivist, vol. 38, no. 4, October 1975, pp. 501-08.

Rendell, Kenneth W: Tax appraisals of manuscript collections. American archivist, vol. 46, no. 3, Summer 1983, pp. 58-69.

Rhoads, J.B.: 'New archival techniques, Archivum, vol. 24, 1977, pp. 77-194.

Rhoads, James B: Role of archives and records management in national information system: a RAMP study (PGI-83/ws/21). Paris: UNESCO, 1983.

Rhoads, James B.: Applicability of unisist guidelines and ISO international standards to archives administration and records management: A RAMP study

(PGI-82 / ws / 4). Paris: UNESCO. 1982.

Rhoads, James B: Alienation and thievery. American Archivists vol. 29, no. 2, April 1966, pp. 197-208.

Rieger, Morris: Modern records retirement and appraisal practice. The Indian Archives, vol. 30, no. 1, January-June 1981, pp. 1-14.

Robbin, Alice: State archives and issues of personal privacy: policies and practices. American Archivist, vol. 9, no. 3, Spring 1986, pp. 163-75.

Roberts, John W: Archival theory: much ado about shelving. American Archivist, vol. 50, no. 1, Winter 1987, pp. 66-74.

Roper, Michael: Directory of national Standards relating to archives administration and records management: a RAMP Study (PGI-86/ws/16). Paris, UNESCO, 1986.

Roper, Micheal: The Changing face of the file: machine-readable records and the archivist. Archives, vol. 1, no. 63, Spring 1980, 145-50.

Russell, Mattie U: The Influence of historians on the archival profession in the United States. American Archivist, vol. 46, no. 3, Summer 1983, pp. 277-85.

Sahli, Nancy: Finding aids: a multi-media systems perpective. American Archivist, vol. 44, no. 1, Winter 1981, pp. 15-20.

Sahli, Nancy: MARC for archives and manuscripts: the AMC format. Chicago, Society of American Archivists, 1985.

Saxena, S.C. (1992): Software Package for libraries, In: advances in Library and Information Sciences, pp. 122-41.

Schellenberg, T.R.: Modern archives: principles and techniques. Melbourne: F.W. Cheshire, 1956.

Schellenberg, T.R.: The future of the archival profession. American Archivist, vol. 22, no. 1, January 1959, pp. 49-58.

Seton, Rosemary E.: Preservation and administration of private archives: A RAMP Study (PGI-84/ws/6). Paris: UNESCO, 1984.

Sheik, Atique Zafar: The academic and educational uses of archives. The Indian Archives, vol. 33, no. 2, July-December 1984, pp. 41-46.

Shiff, Robert A: The archivist's role in records management. American Archivist, vol. 19, no. 2, April 1956, pp. 111-120.

Singh, A.R.: Information management in archives and libraries in India, 18th IASLIC conference, Kurukshetra: 1991, papers, IASLIC, Calcutta.

Singh, A.R. and Rajkumari Shrivastava: Archival libraries collection development in the context of economic recession, 19th IASLIC conference, Ranchi, 1993, papers, IASLIC, Calcutta.

Singh, A.R. and Rajkumari Shrivastava: Information retrieval in archives and archival libraries in india: models and techniques, Indian Archives, Vol. XLI, No. 2, July-Dec., 1992.

Sinha, P.K. (1992): Software for libraries. In advances in library and information science, Vol. 3, pp. 106-15.

Skelton, Robin: The acquisition of literary archives. Archivaria, no. 18, Summer 1984, pp. 214-219.

Slotkin, Helen W. and Lynch, Kaen T: An analysis of processing procedures: the adaptive approach. American Archivists. Archival forms manual. Chicago, Society of American Archivists, 1982.

Smart, John: The professional archivist's responsibility as an advocate of public research. Archivaria, no. 16, Summer 1983, pp. 139-49.

Smith, W.I.: Archives and technology: some experiences of the Public Archives of Canada. The Indian Archives, vol. 33, no. 2, July-Dec. 1984, pp. 1-18.

Smith, Wilfred I: Broad horizons: opportunities for archivists, American Archivists, vol. 37, no. 1, January 1974, pp. 3-14.

Society of American Archivists. Archival forms manual. Chicago, Society of American Archivists, 1982.

Society of American Archivists. Inventories and registers: a handbook of techniques and examplex, Chicago, Society of American Archivists, 1976.

Society of American Archivists: A code of ethics for archivists, Draft 'B', SAA Newsletter, July 1979, pp. 11-14.

Society of American Archivists: A code of ethics for archivists. American Archivist, vol. 43, no. 3, Summer 1980, pp. 415-18.

Sparck Jones, K. and Van Rijsbergen, C.J.: 'Information retrieval test collections', Journal of documentation, vol. 32, 1976, pp. 59-75.

Standards for ethical conduct for rare book, manuscript, and special collections librarians. College and Research Libraries News, vol. 45, July-August 1984, pp. 357-58.

Stapleton, R: Jenkinson and Schellenberg: a comparison. Archivaria, no. 17, Winter 1983-84, pp. 75-85.

Stark, Marie Charlotte: Development of records management and archives services within United Nations agencies: a RAMP study (PGI-ε3/ws/26). Paris: UNESCO, 1983.

Steward, Virginia R: Problems of confidentiality in the administration of personal case records. American Archivist, vol. 37, no. 3, July 1974, pp. 387-98.

Stielow, Frederick J: Subject indexing a large photographic collection. American Archivist, vol. 46, no. 1, Winter 1983, pp. 72-74.

Study on mass conservation techniques for treatment of library and archives material, edited by wolfgang Wachter (PGI-89 / ws / 14). Paris: UNESCO, 1989.

Sung, Carolyn Hoover: Archives and manuscripts: reprography, Chicago, Society of American Archivists, 1982.

Swanson, D.R.: Historical note: Information retrieval and the future of an illusion journal of the American society for information science, vol. 39 (2), 1988, pp. 92-98.

Swets, J.A.: Effectiveness of information retrieval methods. American Documentation, vol. 20 (1) 1969, pp. 72-89.

Sykora, Vojtech: Czechoslovak archives-origin and growth. The Indian Archives, vol. 32, no. 2, July-December 1983, pp, 45-54.

Taylor, Hugh A: Chip monks at the gate: the impact of technology on archives, libraries and the user. Archivaria, No. 33, 1991-92, pp. 177-80.

Taylor, Hugh A.: Archival Services and concept of the user: a RAMP Study (PGI-84/ws/5). Paris: UNESCO, 1984.

Taylor, Hugh A: Archival services and the concept of the user: a RAMP study, Paris, UNESCO. 1984.

Taylor, Hugh A: Clio in the raw: Archival materials and the teaching of history. American Archivist, vol. 23, no. 3-4, July-October, 1972, pp. 317-30.

Taylor, Hugh A: Information ecology and the archives of the 1980s. Archivaria, no. 18, Summer 1984, pp. 25-37.

Taylor, Hugh A: The collective memory: archives and libraries at heritage. Archivaria, no. 15, Winter 1982-83, pp. 118-30.

Taylor, Hugh A: The discipline of history and the education of the archivist. American Archivist, vol. 40, no. 4, October, 1977, pp. 395-02.

Taylor, R.J.: Field appriasal of manuscript collections. Archivaria vol. 1, no. 2, Summer 1976, pp. 44-48.

Tedd, L.A.: An introduction to computer based library systems, Hayden, London, 1977.

Tener, Jean: Accessibility and archives. Archivaria, no. 6, Summer 1978, pp. 16-31.

Thexon, J.E.: Archival potential of machine-readable records in business, American Archivists, vol. 37, 1974, pp. 37-42.

Thorne, R.G.: 'The efficiency of subject catalogues and the cost of information searches', Journal of documentation vol. 11, 1955, pp. 130-48.

Tissing, Robert W. Jr,: The orientation interveiw in archival research. American Archivist, vol. 47, no. 2, Spring 1984, pp. 173-78.

Torchia, M.M.: Two experiments in automated indexing: the Presidential papers and the papers of the Continental Congress, American Archivists, vol. 39, 1976, pp. 437-40.

Van Rijsbergen, C.J.: Informaion retreival, 2nd ed., London, Butterworth, 1979.

Vickery, A, Brooks, H.M. and Robisnon, B. 'A reference and referral system using expert system techniques', Journal of documentation, vol. 43, 1987, pp. 1-23.

Vickery, B.C.: On retrieval system theory, London: Butterworths, 1961.

Vinas, V.: Traditional restoration techniques: a RAMP study: (PGI-88/ws/17). Paris: UNESCO, 1988.

Walch, Timothy: Archives and manuscripts: security. Chicago, Society of American Archivists, 1977.

Walne, Peter: Guide to the archives of International organisation: a RAMP study (PGI-85/ws/18). Paris: UNESCO, 1985.

Walne, Peter: Selected guidelines for the treatment of records and archives: a RAMP study (PGI-90/ws/6). Paris: UNESCO, 1990.

Welch, Edwin: Archival education. Archivaria, no. 4, Summer 1977, pp. 49-59.

Welch, Edwin: Security in an English archive. Archivaria, vol. 1, no. 2, Summer 1976, pp. 49-54.

Weldon, Edward: Archives and the challenges of change. American Archivist, vol. 46, no. 2. Spring 1983, pp. 125-34.

Whyte, Doug: The acquisition of lawyers' private papers. Archivaria, no. 18, Summer 1984, pp. 142-53.

Wilson, Don W: The National Archives: new challenges, new opportunities. Prologue, vol. 19, no. 4, Winter 1987, pp. 220-21.

Wilson, Ian E: 'A noble dream': the origin of the Public Archives of Canada. Archivaria, no. 15, Winter 1982-83, pp. 16-35.

Wilson, Patrick: Situational relevance. Information storage and retrieval, vol. 9, 1973, pp. 457-71.

Wimalaratne, K.D.G.: Scientific and technological information in transactional files in government records and archives: A RAMP study (PGI-84/ws/7). Paris: UNESCO, 1984.

Wurl, Joel: Methodology as outreach: a public mini-cources on archival principles and techniques. American Archivist, vol. 49, no. 2, Spring 1986, pp. 184-86.

Young, Julia Marks, comp: Annotated bibliography on appraisal. American Archivist, vol. 48, no. 2, Spring 1985, pp. 190-216.

# Index

**E**

H



I

**N**

**Q**

**R**

**W**



**Z**